The Perilous Adventures of Time Travel

By Randy Gaddo

Paloma Books   BOOKS   **Ashland, Oregon**

THE PERILOUS ADVENTURES OF TIME TRAVEL
©2021 RANDY GADDO

Published by Paloma Books
(An imprint of L&R Publishing, LLC)

Paloma Books
PO Box 3531
Ashland, OR 97520
www.palomabooks.com

Interior Original Custom Illustrations by Marlon at GetYourBookIllustrations

Interior design: Sasha Kincaid
Cover design: George Deyo

ISBN: 978-1-954163-32-4

Printed and bound in the United States of America
First edition 10 9 8 7 6 5 4 3 2

Author's Note: Characters and events in this book are fictional; however, references to historical events and people are based on documented historical literature, to the best of the author's knowledge. Any references to facts and theories of time travel are based on information gathered through the author's research. It is the author's sincere hope that young (or not-so-young) readers will be encouraged to do their own research on these topics.

1

THE LIONS ARE HUNGRY

SAM SHIFTED HIS GAZE UP FROM the odd-looking remote control device in his hand and was shocked to see in front of him, not twenty feet away, two huge lions drooling at him like he was an appetizer.

Behind the lions, seated in an enormous amphitheater that was unbelievably high, were thousands of people shouting and cheering and pointing their thumbs, some up skyward, some down towards the ground.

Sam felt something heavy pulling at his waist and it seemed like there was a fifteen-pound bowl sitting on his head. He looked down and saw the hilt of an ancient sword hanging in an enormous metal scabbard attached to bronze armor plating on his torso. He reached up and felt a solid metal helmet covering his head and the back of his neck.

Sam realized he wasn't in Massachusetts anymore; or maybe he was having a nightmare that felt too real. He didn't appear to be in his own time zone. Actually, from his study of history, it looked an awful lot like he was in ancient Rome!

He looked up and saw the gaunt, hungry lions, their fierce eyes blazing, beginning to move slowly towards him.

As death appeared imminent, Sam realized it wasn't a dream; this was real. He suddenly grew very calm and oddly enough flashed back to how he had gotten himself into this mess.

Sam, Raven and Akamaru face hungry lions in an ancient Roman amphitheater

2

SAM'S PARENTS ARE MISSING

SAM STEELONNI WAS THIRTEEN YEARS AND seven-months old, but he had already finished high school, was about to graduate from college with a bachelor's degree in technology engineering, and planned to eventually obtain a master's, then a doctorate in physics.

He didn't really need the degrees – he did that because it pleased his parents, who both had multiple doctorates; but mostly he invented things as needed. He enjoyed watching old adventure movies and the 1970s and '80s television shows; he liked to think of himself as a young mix between Angus MacGyver, Indiana Jones and Crocodile Dundee.

Growing up in Boston, Sam tried to downplay his intelligence because he didn't want the "nerd" label; but he'd never been like most other kids. No cartoons, sit-coms, anime, or video games for him – well, maybe a *Roadrunner* cartoon occasionally because he loved the way the Roadrunner out-thought Wiley Coyote and he got a kick out of the coyote's inventions that never worked. No, for him it was the *Discovery Channel*, the *Science Channel*, the *History Channel* – anything that provided ideas, stimulated his inventiveness, or expanded his knowledge of science and history.

His high intellect was based in genetics and in his living environment. His parents had IQs in the 150s and were well known world-wide for their ground-breaking inventions, especially in the physics and genetics field. Their natural sense of curiosity rubbed off on Sam as he grew up around his inquisitive parents.

Sam's IQ rivaled that of his parents. He had his own set of inventions that had gotten their share of attention, such as the solar-powered jet backpack he'd developed when he was eleven years old. It enabled him to fly around the neighborhood and beyond. Oh yeah, that had gotten him all kinds of attention, and not all of it the good kind - like from the Boston police and the Federal Aviation Administration and his parents.

Sam was kind of a loner, not because he wanted to be but because he just found it hard to socially interact with people. He didn't engage in small talk even though he had lots to say.

He would think of things to say but when he tried to verbalize those thoughts his brain didn't always make the connection to his mouth - and he stuttered. He stuh-stuh-stut-stuttered and it embarrassed him, so he generally didn't talk to people unless he absolutely had to.

The cause of stuttering is elusive and often untraceable; his could be rooted in genetics (his mother, Amanda, did stutter when she was younger), or it might just be a random neurological phenomenon.

Either way, his stuttering was improving as he got older; but it still persisted, especially if he was apprehensive. Therefore, in his mind, the important thing was not figuring out how he got it, but finding ways to overcome it. His dad, Tony, had told him everybody has some shortcoming they have to overcome. "That which does not kill you makes you stronger," Tony had said so often that it was embedded in Sam's brain.

There were a few people he could always talk to without stuttering, people he trusted and with whom he was totally comfortable, such as his parents, his college physics professor Dr. Lyonkauph, his best friends Cici and Charger or his pet cat Raven.

Despite his speech impediment and social awkwardness, he still liked to help people. He was the young inventor, helping acquaintances and classmates figure out ways to build better skate ramps, enhanced science projects, create cooler bikes and other helpful items. When he was focused on projects, he didn't stutter as much. When he was helping somebody, he felt more relaxed so he talked more smoothly; so, in a way, it was part of his speech therapy.

The morning he found himself face-to-face with two hungry lions had started pretty much like any other.

He'd gotten up at six a.m. and went to the kitchen to make his breakfast. His parents had normally already been in their home lab for two hours or more working on their most current projects.

So, he'd fix his breakfast of oatmeal mixed with peanut butter and strawberry jam, with fresh strawberries or blueberries and bananas added, and the whole thing slathered with honey. But on this morning there was no oatmeal in the pantry. He had to have oatmeal, so he set off to the lab to ask his mom where there might be some.

His mom and dad were not in the lab. He went down to the basement, where they kept spare equipment and parts. They weren't there either.

Now he was beginning to worry. Where could they be? They rarely left the house before eight or nine o'clock in the morning and if they did they'd leave a note to let him know where they were.

As his eyes scanned through the spare parts on the work bench, they stopped at a strange looking remote control device he'd never seen before. He picked it up, turned it around in his hand and saw the number "2" stamped on it. A large green button had "Send" engraved on it, a red button read "Home." There was a small digital screen that read "AD 80" with a thumb dial below it. Sam knew that AD meant *anno Domini (in the year of the Lord)*, so AD 80 was more than 2,000 years ago, but he had no idea why it was showing on this device.

His stomach growled so he shrugged and continued wandering down the workbench as he absentmindedly put the remote in his right hand into the large pocket of his baggy cargo-shorts. He continued to ferret through the parts, but nothing else caught his interest, so he headed back upstairs.

"Raven," he called loudly. "Raven, come here boy!" Raven was a thirty-five pound result of his parents' experiments with DNA and gene blending; a one year old Siamese Tiger, combining Siamese cat and white Bengal tiger DNA. He was a handsome cat with piercing blue almond-shaped eyes and thick, tawny brown fur highlighted with streaks of white and dark stripes. When Sam had seen the one-of-a-kind test-tube kitten a year earlier he had instantly bonded with him, and his parents finally gave in to his pleas to keep him.

Sam heard Raven bounding through the house before he saw him. The big cat bumped into furniture, his claws clicking and sliding across wood and tile floors to find his best buddy in the world, Sam. Raven thought it might be time to eat. Of course, Raven always thought it was time to eat, just like Sam did. Only Raven didn't eat regular cat food. He had more of a taste for fresh meat, preferably red meat, but any meat would do.

"Where's Mom and Dad buddy?" Sam asked the cat when he finally skidded around the last corner and banged sideways into Sam's knees, nearly knocking him over. He looked up into Sam's eyes and swished his long tail playfully into Sam's face, thinking he could lure his human into a game of chase. Raven's tail had a mind of its own and was constantly in motion, even when the cat slept. It was like a living being who often acted separately from its host.

But Raven – and his tail - could see that his friend was worried. He wished he could ask him what was wrong, but Sam didn't know how to speak cat language.

"Come on boy, we need to find Mom and Dad," Sam said to Raven. "Let's tear this house apart until we find them."

Raven didn't know exactly what was going on, but he did like the part about tearing the house apart. He was really good at that.

Sam and Raven proceeded to search the house from top to bottom and all over the outside, but there was no sign of his parents. Sam called both their cell phones but got an annoying "call cannot be completed" message. Wherever they were, it must be out of range of cell towers, he thought, making their disappearance even more disturbing.

"I'm running out of ideas," Sam said to Raven, as they sat on the couch in the basement lab, considering their options. "How about you come up with the answer."

Raven bounced off the couch and bolted up the stairs to the laundry room, where there was an old cardboard box filled with things dearest to him in the world. He pawed in the box for a second or two, tossing aside old bones, a rubber chicken, a twisted ball of yarn, then took a spongy rubber ball in his mouth and propelled himself back down the stairs. He leaped into Sam's lap and shoved the ball in his face.

"Hey, what are you doing?" Sam asked, shocked by the assault. He took the ball and turned it over in his hand, seeing that it had "BIT" printed on the reverse side. BIT was the acronym for Boston Institute of Technology, a high-tech firm that his parents had founded twenty years ago to fabricate all their inventions.

"You're right!" Sam exclaimed. "You know, sometimes I really think you are smarter than me. Of course! Let's go to Mom and Dad's lab at BIT and see if they're there, or if we can find any clues." Sam didn't know why he hadn't thought of that! It must be the stress of skipping breakfast.

Sam's home was about three miles from the BIT complex. The quickest way he could get there now would be his bike. He went to the garage and took his custom-built bike down from the waist-high pegs where it hung on the garage wall. The bike was one of Sam's first innovations. It had a small motor attached to a frame over the back wheel. The motor was connected with chains to a set of gears. When the bike reached five miles per hour by manual pedal power, the motor automatically kicked in, and he could cruise at speeds up to twenty-five miles an hour.

Sam picked up Raven and set him in a specially constructed metal basket between the motor and the bike seat; it had been much easier to do when the cat was a kitten - now, he filled the entire basket. Sam strapped Raven into a custom seat belt, pulled a specially-designed helmet onto the cat's head and fastened the Velcro chin strap.

He strapped on his own helmet, hit the automatic garage door opener button and jumped onto the bike. He peddled from the driveway and within about ten seconds he was at five miles per hour. The quiet, gas motor kicked in and started the oversized all terrain tires humming at high speed.

In less than nine minutes he was hiding his bike and their helmets in the bushes alongside the BIT building that housed his parents' lab. He didn't want to alert anybody to their presence there, so he and Raven went around back of the building to a basement window. The lab had controlled access due to the confidential nature of the work there, but Sam knew some gaps in security.

The window was key-locked. Sam pulled a penlight from his pocket, unscrewed the top and retrieved two six-inch metal rods. He pushed them into the lock slot, twiddled them around a couple times, and heard the satisfying "click" of the lock sliding open. Picking locks was a handy little trick he'd learned courtesy of You-Tube; only to be used in emergency situations and only for good, never for felonious purposes.

He returned the rods to their place and screwed the top back onto the penlight. He always kept the penlight – and like McGyver, a Swiss army knife – in his baggy pockets. He pushed open the top-hinged door and held it for Raven, then crawled in. It was gloomy in the basement and it took a minute for his eyes to get used to the dim light. But, before he could fully see, he heard a deep, rumbling growl that echoed off the concrete walls.

He clicked on the light still in his hand and pointed it in the direction of the growling. The dim circle of light revealed a huge dog that looked like a mix of Mastiff and Saint Bernard and had to weigh at least 120 pounds. Between Sam and the dog stood Raven, growling, with puffed up fur and tail making him look twice as big as he really was.

"Raven, get back!" Sam hissed quietly but firmly, trying not to arouse the dog. Raven wasn't in a listening mood. He was always up for a fight and he wasn't about to let this mutt hurt Sam. He started to slowly advance on the dog, keeping his steely-blue eyes piercing the dog's greenish-brown orbs. He stopped about three feet from the dog, who wasn't backing off one bit. In fact the canine took a menacing, stiff-legged step towards the smaller cat.

Sam didn't know what to do. He sure didn't want to get between the two of them, but at the same time he didn't want them to kill each other.

Then a solution came to mind. He reached into his right pocket, where he always kept emergency packages of smoked beef jerky slices, a tasty between-meal snack. As he pulled the jerky out with his right hand the weird remote control device came with it and Sam deftly caught it in his left hand just in time to save it from falling.

He quickly tore open the jerky pack and ripped the flat, eight-inch meaty treat in half. As soon as he ripped the package open, both animals caught a whiff of the beefy smell. They quickly forgot about each other and turned their attention to Sam.

Now Sam started to wonder if this had been such a good idea. The dog was looking at him like *he* was the jerky treat. He took a piece of the dried meat in each hand and threw them in opposite directions, almost throwing the remote control along with the jerky in his left hand. The dog took after one and Raven pounced on the other.

This gave Sam enough time to grab Raven, push him through a nearby open doorway and squeeze himself through. As he yanked the door shut he saw, in the bobbing flashlight beam, the drooling dog bounding towards him, chomping on what was left of the beef jerky.

As the door slammed shut, Sam felt the hinges creak and the door shudder as the dog hit the door with full force, not being able to abate his headlong charge. Sam turned around and in the wavering beam of his flashlight was dismayed to see that he and Raven had been shut into a janitor's closet.

He heard the dog sniffing at the bottom of the door and imagined him drooling after devouring the jerky.

Sam knew he and Raven couldn't stay locked in this janitor's closet, trapped in here by the large, growling dog outside the door. They had to get out so they could keep looking for clues to his parents' location.

But apparently the dog had other ideas; he was snuffling at the gap under the door and scratching at it like he was trying to dig his way in.

"Raven, we're going to have to make a run for it," he told his buddy, knowing that, as always, Raven would somehow understand every word he said. "I'm going to open the door, throw beef jerky towards the window we came in and when this dog-monster goes for it, you and I are making a beeline for the stairs. Got it?"

To Sam's surprise, Raven looked him dead in the eye and nodded. "Well, that's different," Sam thought. Then, without hesitation, he opened another beef jerky strip, shoved the door hard, poked his head and right arm around the door, waved the jerky in front of the dog's nose and flung it across the room towards the window.

The dog took off after it, enabling Sam to shove the door the rest of the way opened and run stumbling towards the stairs, with Raven darting ahead of him.

He wasn't even close. The mountain-sized dog caught him halfway up the stairs; but instead of grinding his legs into mush with the long, sharp canine teeth in that cavernous mouth, he gently grabbed the loose folds in Sam's shirttail and simply sat down.

Sam stopped in mid-stride, not able to move forward an inch. But, as he jolted to a stop, his shirt ripped and he almost regained his footing to make the final five stairs to the basement door. He grabbed the closest stair tread ahead of him with his right hand.

He planted both feet on the fifth step and reached around behind him with his left hand to dislodge the dog from the piece of dangling shirt; he grabbed the dog's ear instead. Raven, who was now jammed against the closed basement door, flicked his long, agile tail around back of Sam's neck to help pull him forward.

As Sam tensed to make the final lunge, he clenched his hands and accidently hit the large green button on the weird remote control device he had absently been carrying in his left hand.

Suddenly he, Raven and the dog were engulfed in the midst of a swirling tornado filled with sounds of distant thunder, flashing lightning and misty fog that spiraled up where the stairs had been just a second ago. He got dizzy and nauseous. He lost his sense of direction, his sense of balance, and his sense of humor, all at the same time.

He was just thinking how this couldn't get any weirder, when the swirling slowed and turned to misty, dissipating vapor with cascading multi-colored sparkles which, as it cleared, gave Sam his view of the two lions and the agitated crowd in the ancient amphitheater.

3

IN THE ARENA

SAM WAS PULLED OUT OF HIS momentary flashback as the two menacing lions split up, circled to either side of Sam, lowered their heads, and snarled hungrily.

"What the….," Sam started to say, but before he could finish he saw a brownish-tan streak out of the corner of his eye as Raven lunged towards the lions with his best imitation of a roar. The cat was a fraction the size of the lions and he was outnumbered two to one, but his piercing blue eyes and oddly colored fur were enough to stop the lions in their tracks. He was a new and unknown threat, and they were just curious enough to be cautious as they assessed him.

"Raven, get back here," Sam gasped, reaching with both hands to pull the cat back. "We need to get out of here, now."

At the same time, Raven backed slowly away from the lions as he realized he may have been a bit too macho. The lions recognized that he was just another tasty tidbit for lunch. They began their circling once more.

As Raven backed into Sam's legs he pushed Sam back a couple steps until Sam bumped into something behind him. Keeping his eyes on the lions in front of him, Sam reached back with his left hand, touched animal fur, and felt as much as heard the low, rumbling growl.

He tried to remember if lions hunted in packs, like the raptors in the *Jurassic Park* movies. Had he really just grabbed the mane of a third lion? Maybe the two lions in front of him had just been a distraction, to take his mind off the third lion behind him, who would now take him down like a gazelle on the plains of Africa and the other two would descend on him and Raven to rip them apart.

The crowd was going wild.

The frenzied mob of people in the seats of the amphitheater were screaming and waving their hands, jamming their thumbs up to the sky or down to the ground. The roar of the crowd was deafening.

A small part of Sam's mind was trying to remember if "thumbs down" in ancient Roman amphitheater crowd-language meant save the poor guy or let him die. It didn't really matter though, because the lions in front of him were so close now that he and Raven would be torn to shreds before anybody could get to them.

With Raven's eyes glued to the two lions in front of him, Sam thought it would be safe to look behind him. The fact that his hand hadn't yet been ripped off was a promising sign. Maybe the lion behind him wasn't as hungry as the two in front of him obviously were.

As he started to turn his gaze, the growl behind him suddenly turned to a whimper. That wasn't what Sam had expected to hear. He snapped his head around and looked down.

His brown eyes met the greenish-brown orbs of the big dog, now whimpering instead of growling, looking very confused and afraid. The dog still had a shred of Sam's shirt dangling from his mouth.

Sam was as disoriented as the dog. He had just been busting out of a janitor's closet, running up a stairs away from the big dog and now he had two lions in front of him and the dog grasping his shirt as Sam grasped his furry neck.

Then he fingered the weird remote control device, which he strongly suspected wasn't a remote control device at all. He knew his parents had been dabbling with time travel for decades. Maybe they'd finally hit on something. This probably had something to do with their disappearance.

As the two lions in front of him circled closer and closer, with Raven backed against him and with a fist full of dog fur, Sam desperately attempted to hit the green button of the remote device in his left hand. As he did, his thumb slid over the dial accidently spinning it, indiscriminately stopping at AD 1775. Then he hit the green button and held his breath as the lions crouched to attack.

4

FROM THE AMPHITHEATER TO THE AMERICAN REVOLUTION

A SECOND AFTER HE PUSHED THE green send button there was thunder and bright flashes of light and for about 30 seconds Sam, Raven and the dog saw the streaking, swirling tunnel with colorful flashes of lightning that wrapped around them.

Then, everything stopped and the swirling tunnel gradually dissipated into misty smoke with rainbow-colored sparkling dots floating upward in random patterns. Everything was silent for a moment, until they heard gunfire and felt tremors from thunderous explosions.

Sam looked up from the device and this time he and his two furry traveling companions were standing between two lines of men dressed in eighteenth century military uniforms with American Revolutionary War-era muskets and pistols, shooting at each other.

The entire area was clouded over by grayish smoke and there was the unmistakable odor of burnt sulfur and saltpeter emitting from black powder weapons. He knew this because he'd watched his dad in Revolutionary War re-enactments where they fired period-correct weapons, without real ammunition, of course.

"Aw man, what now?" Sam shouted to Raven over the noise. Raven and the dog both looked up at Sam, then at each other and with their eyes asked the same question; Sam didn't see it, but the dog shrugged his shoulders.

As Sam began to take in the war scene before him, he was jolted into reality when something whisked past his left ear. It didn't take a genius to realize it was a real musket ball and that they were in a shooting war.

"Gentlemen, it looks like we've gotten ourselves in the middle of the American Revolutionary War," Sam said out loud to himself as much as to the animals. He was a student of history and quickly noticed that the uniforms on the fighting men were British red on one side and the blues and browns of American colonial soldiers on the other.

Sam knew in an instant that he had to move quickly or die. He lunged left towards a wooded area that could provide cover. Raven and the dog instinctively followed him.

They all hit the ground at the same time, in the same place. Dog fur, cat whiskers and human skin collided into a mass of elbows, paws and tails. They rolled together into a hole that had been made by an artillery shell exploding under thick, low-hanging bushes.

Once they had sorted out their individual body parts, they huddled together peering out from under the bush. Any unfriendliness that had existed between the large dog and the fiery cat was now lost in their shared fear. But, even though aware of the terrible danger, Sam was amazed by what he saw.

He was interested in past wars and especially the Revolutionary War. His parents, both Massachusetts natives, were members of the Sons and Daughters of the American Revolution, as was Sam. He had studied the war extensively and knew details of all the battles. At the present moment, he probably knew more about the strategic situation than the most senior general on the battlefield.

Sam was afraid, but not panicked. This sudden thrust into another time zone, or dimension, or wherever they were, might have thrown others Sam's age into a horrific tail spin. But after years of analytical, scientific approaches to problems, Sam just took it in stride. He was smart, mature beyond his nearly fourteen years, and worked best under pressure, so he would just play it by ear and assess one problem at a time.

In front of Sam and his animal companions was an open field bordered on two sides by trees and bushes. They lay on the eastern side hidden by bushes growing under low-hanging branches of a giant oak tree.

To their left they could see men huddled behind the remains of an old wooden fence at the top of a long, rolling hill. They were all neatly dressed in red military jackets, white trousers and shiny, black leather boots that came up to their knees.

Flying above their heads, unfurling in the wind, was a red, white and blue flag. Sam recognized it from pictures he'd seen in history books and in re-enactments. It was the old British flag that had been designed by King James I (who was also James VI of Scotland). He designed it in 1606 when he inherited the thrones of England and Scotland. It was England's red and white Cross of St. George superimposed over Scotland's Cross of St. Andrew, a red and white X, all superimposed over a blue background.

A sword-wielding commander on a horse shouted, "Form in ranks of three, attach bayonets, load your weapons," rallying the British soldiers to charge across the field. There were some red coated soldiers lying on the ground, not moving, with dark, red splotches on their uniforms that Sam knew must be blood.

On their right, about one hundred yards from the British troops, Sam saw another group of men standing, crouching or kneeling behind a grove of trees, with muskets to their shoulders ready to fire at the word of their commander. Rising above their heads waving gently in the breeze was a flag Sam recognized immediately; the stars and bars, red and white horizontal stripes with a square, blue patch in one corner filled with a circle of thirteen stars. It was the American flag during the revolution.

These soldiers had shabby, unmatched uniforms. Some had blue or grayish coats that looked like the military jackets of the eighteenth century, but faded and tattered. Some had rough leather jackets made from animal hides. Some had hats, some didn't.

Sam looked down at his shirt, which had been a gladiator's chest plate a moment ago, but it wasn't his shirt or the chest plate anymore. He had somehow traveled into a ragged blue uniform of a colonial soldier in the Revolutionary War.

The commander of this colonial group was shouting, "Sharpshooters, prepare to fire but not until you see the whites of their eyes. Let them redcoats come chargin' across an open field. We'll show 'em how it's done here in the colonies."

The battle was at its fiercest and Sam had no intention of getting in the middle of it; but what happened next made him take actions that he never thought he could.

As they lay there watching the battle unfold, Sam saw a flash of blue streak across his vision to the right. He looked in that direction just in time to see a body falling towards him. He tried to scream but his mouth was so dusty and dry only a ragged croak sounding like "Awrrg!" came out of it.

There, in front of him, ten feet away in the battlefield was a boy no older than Sam, dressed in a colonial soldier's uniform. The boy was bleeding profusely from his left shoulder. He was flat on his stomach with his face turned towards Sam. His eyes were opened and Sam could see he was in great pain.

"Help," the boy pleaded to Sam. "Help me."

Before Sam knew what he was doing, he was out on the battlefield, grabbing the boy by his good shoulder, half-dragging, half carrying him to the hole under the oak tree. Sam wasn't exceptionally big or tall – average for his age at five-feet, eight-inches tall and 165 pounds. However, he stayed in really good shape by lifting weights and running circuit courses with his friend Cici. Plus, his adrenaline was kicked into high gear, so pulling the boy out of the line of fire was relatively easy and instinctual.

Even in his pain and nearly unconscious, the boy still clung to his musket in his left hand and the bayonet in his right.

When he got the boy under the tree, Sam knew what he had to do. He was CPR certified and had read many first-aid books. He knew he had to first stop the bleeding. He reached into his back pocket where he always had a large handkerchief. He pulled it out, folded it twice, and then gently pressed it directly on the bleeding hole in the boy's shoulder, causing the boy to wince in pain.

Sam knew that next he had to treat for shock and, clearly, the boy was going into shock. He had to talk to him to keep him awake and alive. Sam was nervous, so he stuttered when he asked, "Whuh, whuh what's your name?"

"Alex," the boy said, "Alex McPherson."

"Do you li- li- live around here?" Sam inquired, taking a couple of deep breaths to calm down so his stuttering would stop.

"Yes, I am from Boston," the boy said, barely able to keep his eyes opened now.

Boston. Of course, Sam thought, again drawing on his vivid memory of books he'd read about the Revolutionary War. He must be at the Siege of Boston; the early phase of the American Revolutionary War, when New England militiamen surrounded Boston to prevent British soldiers there from being able to conduct raids in the nearby countryside. The siege had lasted from April 1775 to March 1776 and eventually General George Washington had led American colonists, who forced the British to withdraw.

Sam snapped back to reality and looked at the boy he had dragged off the battlefield. He knew he had to get the boy to a doctor very soon.

"How old are you?" Sam asked as he looked around to find a way to get the boy out of the war zone.

"Thirteen years, eight months…almost fourteen," the boy said proudly. Sam was shocked. In his world, fourteen-year-old boys were worrying about what's for dinner. In Alex's world, he was worried about whether he would live to see another day.

"I'm gonna' get you to a doctor, Alex," Sam said with false confidence – he had no idea if he could find this guy a doctor.

"Why, it's only a little scratch," Alex said, looking down at his left shoulder with eyes that tried to focus but crossed instead. "Give me a minute or two to rest and I'll get back in the fight."

"Yeah, well, you're not going anywhere except the doctor," Sam insisted, not knowing exactly how was he going to do that. "Do you know where the nearest doctor is?"

"Down the hill and to the right about a mile back at the headquarters," Alex said in a slurred but distinct Bostonian accent.

"OK, then that's where we're going," said Sam, relieved that his stuttering was gone. He had seen plenty of movies where the hero stooped down and threw the injured person over his back and carried him to safety. Only, this wasn't a movie and he wasn't a hero. He didn't even know if he could make it that mile himself without getting shot, let alone carry the injured soldier.

He had to use his head. Think. Transportation, that's what he needed. He swept his glance from side to side and then he spotted it. It was crude, but it would do.

Off to his right about fifty feet, sheltered out of gunshot range behind a clump of bushes, he saw the back end of a small wagon, with the word "ammunition" written on the back. Hoping it wasn't full of explosives, he dashed to it.

Not only was it empty, but attached to the front of the wagon was a small but rugged little donkey, which now looked fearfully over his shoulder and brayed at Sam as if to say, "Get me the heck out of this war zone!"

"Perfect," Sam said to himself. Then he raced back to Alex and said, "Hey soldier, we're gonna' get you out'ta here." Before Alex could protest, Sam reached down and pulled him into a seated position. He hoisted Alex to his feet, put his uninjured arm over his shoulder and half-dragged, half-carried the wounded boy, still holding his musket and bayonet, towards the wagon. Raven and the dog didn't need an invitation to join them. In fact, as soon as they heard the donkey bray they seemed to understand him, bounded ahead and were in the wagon before the two boys had crossed half the distance. The donkey didn't really welcome these new intruders, but he was in no position to argue as he was lodged into a corner, blocked to his front by heavy vines and bushes.

Now Sam faced another dilemma. As he stood alongside the wagon, he realized there was no way to hoist Alex over the side of the wagon and gently deposit him without causing more pain and suffering.

He crouched down and set Alex on his feet. Alex hooked his right elbow over the side of the wagon and balanced himself while Sam went to the rear of the wagon and dropped the tailgate. Before Sam could get back to him, Alex was already moving towards the back of the wagon, but he only got two or three steps before he started to stagger. Sam caught him just before he toppled and guided him to the rear of the wagon, helped him into a seated position and then pushed him toward the front of the wagon.

"Lay down," Sam ordered Alex, then covered him with an old horsehair blanket that was in the wagon. Now he'd have to see if he knew how to drive one of these things.

"Hey, since I have the opposable thumbs, I'll drive," he said flippantly to Raven and the dog, which for now he'd call "dog" but who still needed a name. He'd read books where the hero interjected humor during tense times. But since there was nobody but him and wounded Alex and three animals, his attempt to lighten the mood fell flat – almost; Sam didn't see Raven roll his eyes skyward and the dog shake his head.

Sam hoisted himself into the driver's seat, wondering to himself, do you call someone who drives a wagon a driver, or a wagoneer? He'd have to look that up when he got home…if, he got home.

He grabbed the reins that were attached to the harness around the donkey's body. The donkey looked back over his shoulder at Sam and awaited instructions.

"HeeYah!" said Sam. The donkey blinked. "Mush," Sam tried again. Two blinks this time. "Move, you stupid donkey," Sam said in frustration as he pulled hard right on the reins, trying to get the donkey out of the mess of bushes and vines.

To his surprise, the donkey started turning, moving forward and right at a fast clip, throwing Sam backwards. He regained his composure and tried to guide the donkey, who now seemed to be in charge.

"He knows where to go," a voice behind Sam said. Sam glanced back and Alex was gazing at him with half-opened eyes. Alex's face was pale white and it looked like he was having lots of trouble keeping his eyes opened.

"He's the company donkey," said Alex sleepily. "He knows home is in that direction. Let him go." Then Alex passed out.

Sam did as Alex said and just let the donkey guide the wagon. In about five bumpy minutes they were pulling into a military encampment filled with tents and bustling with activity. A flag in the middle of the camp flew the Colonial colors. The donkey stopped abruptly in the middle of the camp.

"Heh, heh, help!" shouted Sam, angry at himself for stuttering. "Suh, suh, suh, somebody, I've got a wounded boy…uh, I mean soldier here." Everybody was running around, but nobody heard him. He stood up in the wagon and shouted at the top of his lungs. "Hey, is there a doctor around here!"

That did the trick. An overall-clad man who didn't look too much older than Sam rushed to the side of the wagon and said, "What's wrong with him?" Sam didn't have time to explain things to a young farm boy. "Get me a doctor," he yelled at the boy.

"I *am* the doctor!" the boy shouted back.

"You?" said Sam, now noticing that the boy had blood on his hands and his shirt, probably from helping others.

Before the boy could answer, Sam was jerked around by a huge hand on his left shoulder and a ten-pound musket as long as he was tall, with bayonet attached, was thrust into his hands. He looked up into a face he had seen in many history books.

"Get back on the front line soldier," ordered the man, who was astride a powerful, white horse. Sam saw stars on the collar of his dusty blue jacket. "You did a fine job getting this soldier to safety. You saved his life, now get back to the fight. We need every able-bodied man out there."

Sam couldn't believe his eyes. He was being ordered by General George Washington, who had assumed command of the newly-formed Continental Army in June 1775. He would later be the first American president starting in 1789.

Sam grabbed the musket and screamed, "Yes Sir!" as he glanced at Alex and saw that the doctor was taking care of him. Sam jumped off the wagon, and with Raven and the dog at his heels, he began to run towards the front line; but, when he was out of sight he veered off to anywhere that wasn't the front line. As he ran, he cast aside the musket and fished into his pocket to pull out the odd remote control device, which he now knew was much more than it appeared to be.

He ran toward the closest clump of bushes, hit the ground, threw one arm around Raven and the other around the dog and without really thinking, hit the red "Home" button.

Everything went into slow motion. It was as though they had again stepped into the eye of a swirling tornado. Circling around them were scenes of bloody battle, cannons thundering, people screaming, flashes of lightning and rifles firing volley after volley. Then the tornado went totally black with sparkles of red, green, blue and yellow drifting around them. Gradually, the blackness started to turn cloudy white with sparkles and he could see he was back in his parents' home laboratory. Hitting the red button had done the trick; he had found the way home once again.

He looked at Raven and the dog, who looked back at him through dazed eyes filled with the same shocked relief that they were back in familiar territory.

Now he needed to figure out what was going on, what had happened to his parents, and how he was going to find them. He knew he needed help and he knew exactly who to call.

5

FINDING REINFORCEMENTS

SAM AND THE ANIMALS WERE EXHAUSTED and the adrenaline wore off when they all slumped into the big, comfy sofa. Sam was in the middle, Raven was curled up on his right and the dog had his massive head on Sam's left knee. Raven's animated, never-sleeping, twitching tail lay across both of them. They all feel asleep in an instant.

After a couple of hours Sam was the first to wake as he came out of a dream where a lion was about to take his head off. Had it all been a dream? It had to be. There was no way that his day had gone that far out of whack.

But reality smacked him in the face when he glanced down and saw the dog, who by now had his giant, drooling head fully across Sam's leg. That dog didn't belong here; it belonged at BIT, so Sam knew he hadn't imagined it all.

It started coming back to him – the arena, the lions, the crowd, the injured Colonial boy, George Washington…the weird remote control device! He panicked a little. Where was it? It had been in his hand. Now it wasn't.

He took a quick glance left, then right, and relaxed when he saw it safely tucked between the seat cushions. "I'm going to lose this just like dad loses the TV remote," Sam said to the two animals, who both jerked their heads up at the sound of his voice. He could tell they were dazed and confused too.

But hunger quickly overpowered confusion as all three realized they were starving. "Come on guys, let's get some chow," Sam said to them. He was surprised to see both of them get up and head straight to the kitchen as if they had understood every word he'd said.

Rummaging through the fridge Sam found a whole, two-day old pepperoni and sausage pizza. He ripped off a slice and chomped half of it as the dog peered up at him with hungry eyes and drooled. Sam tossed him a slice and the dog deftly caught and swallowed it almost without chewing.

Reaching back into the fridge Sam pulled out a piece of raw calf liver, Raven's favorite food, and laid it in a plate on the floor. Raven was more deliberate about eating than the dog, choosing to rip a piece of meat off and chew it carefully, keeping one foot on the liver, claws gripping it as he eyed the dog suspiciously.

The dog showed no interest, he just wanted more pizza. So as the three of them silently filled their bellies, Sam started considering his next moves.

First, he had to get a better grip, literally and figuratively, on this weird remote control device and how it worked. He knew it was the key to finding his parents but he didn't know how or why. He noticed a circular tab with a hole molded into the remote's metal exterior and realized what it was for.

He rummaged in the kitchen junk drawer, which contained myriad items that didn't belong somewhere else, until he found the chain he was looking for. It was about twelve inches long with a spring snap on one end and a leather loop on the other. The nickel-plated chain was the type bikers or cowboys wore to prevent pick-pockets from stealing their wallet. Sam had no idea where it had come from; it had been in the drawer forever, just waiting to be used.

He attached the spring snap to the remote's tab, then unbuckled his belt and pulled it out of the first two loops on his right side, slipped the chain's leather loop over the belt and pulled it back far enough so he could re-thread the belt back through the loops. He buckled his belt and slipped the remote into his right pocket.

The animals had been watching with mild interest, lazy after gorging themselves. Sam saw them staring at him and started to explain, "Now I won't have to worry about accidently losing the remote again…" but he stopped when he realized they wouldn't understand.

He needed help and the first person he thought of was Cecelia McSimmons, or Cici as he called her. He had known Cici since they were both toddlers and she was his best friend. They had a lot in common. She was incredibly smart and her parents were physicists who worked with his parents at BIT. They went to the same schools growing up; she was nearly finished getting her bachelor's degree at the same college he attended. She was an accomplished inventor in her area of expertise, artificial intelligence. They liked the same kinds of movies and TV series; she identified with Veronica Mars, Lydia Martin in *Teen Wolf* and Zena Warrior Princess.

Lately Sam started to realize that she was also becoming a very attractive girl. She was filling out in all the right places, and although he didn't want to, he couldn't help but just stare at her sometimes when she wasn't looking.

Sam stood up and said, "All right you guys, I have to call Cici so I want the two of you to stay here in case Mom and Dad get back. Raven, I want you and, uh, *the dog*, to get along."

"*The dog* has a name," said a deep, rumbling voice. Sam whipped around in a deft 360-degree spin, his eyes flitting to see who had said it. "My name is Akamaru," the voice rumbled, and this time Sam saw where it was coming from, but he couldn't believe his eyes. He thought he actually saw the dog's lips moving when he said the words.

Sam stuck his hands into his pants pockets; then took them out, crossed his arms, took a deep breath, tilted his head a bit to the left, and tried to casually respond to this latest shock to his world. "So whuu-whuu what kind of name is Akamaru?" he asked the dog, mentally kicking himself for stuttering. He watched closely to see if the animal's lips moved again; they did!

"I was named by the young son of the BIT janitor," the dog responded just as casually. "Akamaru was a character on one of his favorite series on the Cartoon Network, called *Naruto*. The janitor's family took me in as a puppy but when I got bigger they didn't have room in their small home, so he stuck me in the basement at BIT. I hate it there! I'm like a prisoner."

Sam was impressed by the dog's communication skills; it was like talking with an intelligent human. "So, since the janitor works for my parents and they own BIT, technically you are a member of the BIT family, thus you could belong here!" Sam rationalized.

"Hmmm, interesting, I like where you're going with this..." Akamaru said, sitting down and bringing a paw up to rub his chin in a contemplative, human-like gesture. "I really don't think anybody there will miss me."

Raven had been watching this exchange like it was a tennis match, his mouth hanging open, his head snapping back and forth, eyes wide, tail flicking. In a lilting baritone voice he asked, "Hey, how come he can understand you, but he can't understand me?" he asked Akamaru. "I've been wishing I could get him to understand cat language all my life and he hasn't gotten it yet!"

When Raven spoke Sam pivoted, twirled his hands out in a magician's gesture, bowed slightly, and said in a sing-song voice, "Tada! It looks like you got your wish buddy, because I just understood every word you said."

The three of them were silent for a long moment, looking back and forth at each other as they let this latest development sink in. Then, almost as if on cue, all three burst out laughing – yes, laughing – which shocked Sam even more because he didn't know animals laughed.

"Somehow," he said as he took a deep breath, coughed a little, and got his laughing under control. "Somehow, it appears that when the three of us were touching as we went through that time tunnel or vortex or whatever it was, our brains got in sync and now we can understand each other."

"It will make communicating much easier as we try to find your parents," said Akamaru; then, with a touch of sarcasm in his voice, he asked Sam, "So what's our next move *genius*?"

Sam was a little surprised that a dog could be sarcastic; but then there were many surprising things happening, so he just shook it off and took it in stride.

"I need to call Cici," he said, not looking as he reached into his pocket for his cell phone and pulled out the remote control device instead, the new attached chain rattling as he did. He almost started to dial until he realized what he was doing. Akamaru looked at him with raised eyebrows and Raven yowled, "Boss, don't push that button again!"

He stopped abruptly, realized what he was about to do, and said, "Thanks guys, it's going to be good to have you two watching my back." Then he went to find his phone so he could call in the cavalry, in the form of Cici.

6

CICI TO THE RESCUE

As Sam searched for his cell phone, Cecilia McSimmons was several blocks away in the workshop she'd created in the bonus room on the third floor of her parents' home. The workshop was her space, her inner sanctum, the place where everything was in order, everything was in its place, and she knew exactly where each and every item was.

Though she was only thirteen years old, she had been refining her workshop for more than five years. The room was big, about fifteen feet wide and almost twice as long. The walls were painted hot pink and fluorescent green – her favorite colors - and the floor was overlaid in vinyl that looked like hardwood, enabling Cecilia to roll anywhere on her six-wheeled, rotating work chair.

She organized her space so precisely that she could almost work in total darkness and still find what she needed. Each piece of advanced equipment on eighteen tables, each tool right down to tiny screw drivers and wrenches, had its own place to live. This precise organization ensured her highest work efficiency.

The four-by-eight foot, white, heavy-duty plastic tables lined the entire perimeter of the room, each holding different electronic and digital equipment and tools. A wide-opened space in the middle enabled Cecilia to propel herself on her chair from one side to the other, or end-to-end, by planting her feet on the floor and pushing with her powerful legs.

Cecilia kept her legs – and the rest of her body – in good physical shape. She pictured herself as Zena, Warrior Princess – strong and confident. She had long legs and standing at five-feet, seven-inches, she was fairly tall for her age. She got height from her father's side of the family; he was over six feet tall and his two brothers were taller than him.

From her mother, Cecelia had inherited fiery, auburn-red shoulder-length hair that had a mind of its own no matter what she tried to do; it curled and flared around her face like the red rays of an angry sun. Most of the time she kept it pulled back in a ponytail or she'd try to contain it by pulling a colorful elastic headband over the unruly mass of curls.

Cecilia stayed strong by doing all kinds of unusual workouts. She researched the training of elite groups of warriors such as U.S. Marines or Navy SEALS and modeled her workouts after theirs.

She and her dad, who served one four-year tour in the Marines (and once a Marine, always a Marine), had built an obstacle course on their ten-acre estate. It was exactly like the one at the fabled Marine Corps Recruit Depot, Parris Island, in South Carolina where young men and women trained to become U.S. Marines.

The course consisted of several challenging obstacles using ropes, logs, steel bars and walls designed to challenge a person's strength, endurance, stamina, and coordination. She could run the course in just under five minutes, which was near the time any Marine recruit had ever run it. Someday, she thought she might like to accept the challenge of becoming a Marine.

Though she didn't really know or think about it, she was beautiful. Her stunning auburn hair was complemented by creamy bronzed skin, blazing blue eyes, full red lips, a small, turned up nose, and beautiful white teeth. She was just becoming aware that her body was transforming from a skinny kid to a shapely young woman.

However, she rarely took time to think about her looks because she was constantly in her workshop engaged in several projects at once. She was a consummate multi-tasker. When she walked through the door of her workshop, she instantly immersed herself in her projects, most of them dealing with advanced AI, or artificial intelligence. She had the smarts to do it too. She had already breezed through high school and was near graduating from college with a bachelor's degree in AI; she planned to continue with her education until she obtained her doctorate. AI was her passion. She envisioned a world where AI equipment, or robots as her old-school dad called them, would serve mankind in every aspect of life. Ultimately, her goal was to construct a walking, talking robot that looked, felt and acted like a human.

As Sam was at his house preparing to speed-dial Cecilia's number, she was in the middle of a very delicate procedure to activate her latest project. It was her first attempt to incorporate life-like traits into an artificially-intelligent being – in this case, the being took the form of a pot-bellied pig.

She had always wanted a pet pig because they are smart and cute, but never felt she had the time to take care of one. So, she decided to create a maintenance-free pet. She had taken a few liberties in her design that wandered from Mother Nature's living example.

Her AI pig, named Lily-Rose after her two favorite flowers, was the cutest thing she'd ever seen. Weighing in at about fifty pounds, Lily-Rose stood two-feet tall and three-feet long. She had pink synthetic vinyl skin covered with soft white, fibrous synthetic hair that was thick and long enough to actually brush smooth. She had a black-and-pink turned up piggy nose, large, beautiful eyes that turned different colors depending on her "mood" and long, black eyelashes that batted and blinked.

Cici had also added a few enhanced features. Lily-Rose's curly-cue tail had a small LED light and a camera in the tip so she could see 360 degrees all around and zoom in or out. Her piggy nose was also a variable-strength stun gun, capable of twelve- to 300,000-volts, so she could deliver a gentle warning shock or rock somebody's world.

She could also expel tear gas up to thirty feet, appropriately, from her derriere. Cici wanted to ensure the little pig could defend herself. Part of the reason she'd lovingly constructed Lily-Rose was that Cecelia envied Sam for having Raven. She watched Sam and Raven playing and interacting with each other and she longed for a pet that she could be that close to.

Sam was her best friend – one of her only friends, really. She didn't make friends easily. She wasn't like most girls her age and she didn't identify with them. She always felt like she had been born into the wrong time period. She was an old soul who could have lived happily a hundred years in the past.

Sam was the only boy she would hang out with. She knew other guys and lately she noticed that they seemed to pay more attention to her, but she had no interest in them. Compared to Sam, other guys seemed pretty – well, pretty boring, really.

She and Sam went way back. They were buddies since she could remember, but lately she felt like she would like to see him all the time, every day. She and Sam were very different. Where she was highly organized and structured, he was footloose and fancy free; not that he was disorganized or negligent, but he tended to be more prone to act first and think later.

He used to be a skinny kid with a mass of thick, black, unkempt hair, always wearing cargo shorts and T-shirts with some corny saying such as "Quiet please, genius at work" or "Nerds do it smarter." But then he started to work out with her and she noticed that he was transforming from a skinny kid to – and she blushed when she thought about it – but he was really starting to be sort of a hunk.

His arm muscles were starting to pop out from under his shirt sleeves and the legs that emerged from the cargo shorts were striated and they pulsed and popped as he walked. His shoulders had gone from hunched and skinny to broad and hard and his well-defined chest sloped down to flat abs that were beginning to show a six-pack.

At first she had been able to beat him running the obstacle course, but once he got the hang of it, he blasted through it a full minute faster than she could. She impressed him by doing multiple sets of forty perfect pushups and fifteen pull-ups, but before long he was doing twice that many.

Then he started going to a men's barber shop and getting great haircuts. Trimmed up and styled, his jet-black hair, dark Italian skin and his deep, brown eyes with long, dark eyelashes made him look – and she shuttered again – made him look kind of sexy.

Cecilia – or Cici, which is what Sam called her and he was the only person in the world who called her that – and she liked it – pushed aside the distracting thoughts as she re-focused on the final procedure to activate Lily-Rose. She double-checked the systems on her calibration equipment, saw all green lights and poised her index finger over the button that read, in capital letters, "ACTIVATE."

Just as her finger was almost touching the button, her phone rang. She glanced down and saw Sam's face come up on her video call screen and he said the code word they had used for years to tell each other that this was an emergency situation.

"REDRUM!" Sam said to her in an urgent tone. REDRUM was from the Steven King book and movie entitled *The Shining*. It had been uttered by the young son of a man driven mad by spirits in a haunted house and when read backwards in a mirror the word spelled "MURDER."

"Cici, my parents are missing and I've discovered something that will blow your mind, you need to get over here ASAP!" Sam said to her in a tense, worried tone that instantly got her attention.

She pulled her finger back from the ACTIVATE button and said to Sam, without hesitation, "I'll be there in a few minutes."

She turned to go, but stopped and went back to the still lifeless Lily-Rose. "I can't leave you here one push of a button away from life," Cici said to the inanimate pig. She had programmed the AI animal to walk…and talk. She had pre-loaded the pig's small but massive-capacity hard-drive with encyclopedic knowledge and information and tons more capacity to learn. Lily-Rose would develop by experiencing the real world, just as a flesh-and-blood animal would – after all, Cici had reasoned, the brain is just nature's computer.

Without hesitation, Cici pushed the activation button. There was a click as the hard-drive engaged, some humming as the operating system kicked in and transmitted initiation codes. The first sign of life came from Lily-Rose's eyes, currently a beautiful lavender color with jet-black irises. The pig's long eyelashes flicked up and down twice, then her eyes smoothly rolled up and saw Cici.

"Hi mom," Lily-Rose said in a soft, raspy, whisper as she oriented her synthetic vocal cords to simulate speech; that would also improve with time and practice. "It's nice to finally meet you."

Cici was ecstatic. She brought her right hand to her mouth and gasped. "Holy moly, it worked! It lives…" she said, putting her hand down to stroke Lily-Rose's head.

"Hmmm, am I *it* or am I *she*," the pig asked, already starting to question her existence. "After all, you did pattern my thoughts to your own, so really I am…you…in piggy form…"

Cici stepped back, grinned and considered this. After a few moments, she giggled and said, "You're right, you are not *it*, you are *she*…and yes, I used my own thought process to program yours, but you also have the capacity to learn, develop and be your own person… or rather, your own pig…or whatever…"

"OK mom, I get it," Lily-Rose said, rolling her eyes and sounding a little like a petulant 'tween.

"Don't call me mom. I'm not your mom…well, I guess technically I am since I made you…but I'd rather just be your friend. You can call me Cecelia."

"OK Cecelia, I'd like that. You can call me Lily-Rose. So, what do we do next?"

Cici was so excited she could hardly contain herself, but the pig's question reminded her that Sam needed her ASAP. "Well, Lily-Rose, interesting you should ask because we have to scoot on out of here and go help my friend Sam with a problem he has. Can you walk?"

Lily-Rose took a tentative step, then another, then walked across the thirty-foot room, pivoted with an intentional swish of her synthetic-pork butt and walked back. Then she turned and ran across the room and back…fast, stopping on a dime at Cici's feet. "I think I've got the hang of it," she said with a perfect smile showing off her pearly-white, human-like teeth; her eyes now swirled with green and pink, matching the room's colors.

"Okey dokey, I do believe you are right," Cici said, impressed with the pig's progress. "So, let's hit the road to Sam's"

7

SAM TELLS IT ALL

TRUE TO HER WORD, CICI RAN the six blocks from her house to Sam's in less than two minutes, with Lily-Rose at her heels, and was barely even out of breath when she burst through his front door without knocking. Sam wasn't the kind to overreact to situations so Cici knew that when he called with that tone of voice, and used the code word, there was a real emergency.

"I got here as quick as I could what's…" she said as she started towards Sam but stopped when she heard a deep, rumbling growl and saw the massive dog that was sitting at Sam's feet rise and walk towards her stiff-legged, head down, drooling.

Lily-Rose instinctively leaped between the dog and Cici and let out an ear-splitting squeal, her eyes a blazing red inferno. A bolt of white-hot lightning arced across her nose from one nostril to another. Her formerly perfect teeth were now exposed in her snarling mouth but they'd grown and sharpened, now looking like a vampire's…another little security feature Cici had thrown in for good measure.

"Back off mutt or feel the wrath of my nose," Lily-Rose said in a gravely rasp.

"Hey, hey, everybody be cool, it's OK Aka, stand down, she's a friend," Sam said to Akamaru. Sam had a habit of shortening names to save time. He sometimes abbreviated Raven's name to Rave. "Akamaru, meet Cecilia McSimmons and…and, um, who is this exactly?"

"Lily-Rose, it's OK," Cici said, a little embarrassed by her new sidekick's introductory episode. Lily-Rose backed up a step, unsharpened her teeth, turned her eyes back to pink and green and sat down. Cici gave Sam an abbreviated history of the pig, then said, "Lily-Rose, this is Sam, Raven and...what is his name?"

"Akamaru...it's a long story..." Sam said when he saw the question about the unusual name forming in Cici's eyes; he and Cici often were able to anticipate what the other was going to say before they said it.

The dog immediately backed up a step and sat down awkwardly, happy for an excuse to back off. This pig looked dangerous. He said, "Hi Cecilia, sorry, didn't mean to upset you or your friend. I'm a bit jumpy after the day we've had so far. It's good to meet you."

Sam heard that, but all Cici heard was the dog making some woofing and yowling sounds as she saw his mouth move like he was trying to tell her something. She didn't understand because she hadn't been through the time vortex – not yet, anyway.

"Hi Akamaru," she said as she reached down to let the dog sniff her hand, hoping he wouldn't chomp it off in response. Instead, he put his paw under her hand and gently pressed his dog lips onto it; she cringed a little – it was just a tiny bit creepy. She swore it looked like he was kissing it as he looked up at her and gave a couple more woofs, which translated to "enchante`"- French for "Nice to meet you." Sam was again amazed at what these animals were capable of doing and saying.

"Well, he's a friendly beast, isn't he," Cici said to Sam as she pulled her drool-covered hand away, wiped it on her shorts and patted the dog on the head.

Akamaru looked at Sam and woofed/said, "She's a real dish Sam. I think I'm in love."

Lily-Rose understood everything the dog said, because she had a universal language translator modem attached on her hard drive, which enabled her to translate any language. So she tapped Cici's knee, motioned with her hoof for her to lean down and whispered into her ear, telling her everything the dog had said. Cici blushed slightly, stood up, arched her left eyebrow and gave the dog a stern, but appreciative, glance.

Sam ignored Akamaru and said to Cici, "Yeah, he's a real gentleman, but now that everybody is introduced can we get back to the problem at hand?"

"Oh, yeah, sure, so your parents are missing? What do you think happened to them? Did you look everywhere? Have you tried calling them? And what is this amazing thing you've discovered that will blow my mind?" Cici fired off the questions in a machine gun staccato that left Sam with his mouth opened trying to answer, but not getting in a word edgewise.

"Stop!" he exclaimed, so loudly that it caused Cici to snap her mouth shut and just stare wide-eyed at Sam with a shocked look on her face. Sam almost never spoke loudly to her, never yelled at her, so when he did it now she knew he was really stressing out.

"Sorry," he said in a normal tone, "I didn't mean to yell; I'm just on edge and when I tell you about this you'll understand why. Come and sit down and let me start from the beginning. I really need your help."

Sam and Cici sat on the couch with the three animals sitting on the floor in front of them. Cici swore they were listening as Sam proceeded to tell her about his day. She was tracking along calmly when he told her about his breakfast issues and looking for his parents and going to their lab and finding the dog; but when he got to the part about the lions in the Colosseum, it was her turn to raise her voice.

"Whoa, stop, get back!" she said as she held up her hand like a school crossing guard stopping traffic. "You are trying to tell me that you think you were actually in a Roman amphitheater circa AD 80 and that there were real lions there?" she squawked, her voice cracking, her throat suddenly dry, as she thought maybe Sam was having some sort of breakdown. "Are you sure you weren't dreaming, Dorothy?" she chided him, making reference to Dorothy in the *Wizard of Oz*.

Sam looked at her like she'd kicked him in the gut. She realized that Sam, who usually traded pithy barbs with a good sense of humor, was not in a joking mood.

"OK, so this wasn't a dream, please continue," she said, determined to let him talk until he got it all out.

So, he went on with the tale, through his other time jump to the Revolutionary War, meeting George Washington, then finding his way home and lastly, about how he could now talk to the animals.

Her mind was screaming, "OMG Sam has fallen off the deep end and can't get back up!" When Sam finished, he just stopped and looked at her in wide-eyed distress.

Cici remembered her dad's advice about tense situations. "Take a minute, count to ten, take a few deep breaths before you say anything," he'd told her a thousand times until it was etched into her brain. "If you don't, what comes out of your mouth may not be what you thought was in your brain."

So she did count to ten, she did take two or three deep breaths, then her searing blue eyes met his deep brown eyes and she could see that, regardless of whether what he told her actually happened or it was some kind of *Wizard of Oz* dream, he believed it to be true, so she needed to work from there.

"OK," she said calmly, "I believe you. Now we need to figure out where we go from here."

She immediately saw the figurative cloud that was hanging over his head dissipate, lift and allow the sunlight to shine again. His eyes brightened and she could see that wonderful brain of his start to churn.

"So your theory is that your parents have been secretly working on time travel and somehow have left our time zone or dimension and gotten lost in another one?" she asked Sam.

"Well, when you put it that way, it does sound pretty crazy, but yes, that is exactly what I'm saying. The problem is, I'm not sure exactly when or where they are and I am not familiar with their experiments so I don't really understand how to work this thing," Sam said as he pulled the remote control from his pocket, careful this time not to push any buttons.

Luckily, each button and the dial were recessed into a pocket that prevented them from being pushed when in his pocket. Otherwise, he might have accidently sent himself to who-knows-where-or-when. Still, he thought some sort of flip cover over the buttons and dial would be a good idea. He added that task to a mental checklist of things to do.

"Knowing your parents they must have kept detailed notes on their work. Why don't we see if we can find them," Cici suggested.

Sam slapped his forehead lightly with the palm of his hand and shook his head as he said, "Ya' see, that is why I got you involved. I knew you'd hone-in on a solution. Of course, that's what we need to do! And I think I know where we can start looking for their notes."

As he was talking Sam slipped the remote back into his pocket, launched off the couch, grabbed Cici's hand and propelled the two of them towards the basement lab. Raven, Akamaru and Lily-Rose didn't need an invitation; they fell in behind the two humans as the five of them flew down the stairs.

8

STUCK IN TIME

As the two young adults, two animals and one AI pig made their way to the basement in the present time, Sam's parents, Anthony "Tony" and Amanda Steelonni, were huddled behind a pile of woven wicker baskets in an alleyway somewhere in Rome, AD 80.

The two physicists had been dabbling in the concept of time travel for decades. However, it was purely by good fortune that they discovered the one key ingredient which propelled them from theory to reality; and, from modern-day Boston to ancient Rome. Unfortunately, they overlooked some important facts in the process.

During an expedition in India they found a glowing, unknown, unearthly element that was believed to inexplicably alter the human physiology and cause the body to vibrate beyond the speed of light. They had been seeking evidence for a theory they were developing, that ancient scientists had somehow obtained the ability to travel through time.

Of course, they were the only people who knew their true reason for setting up and funding the expedition. It had cost a pretty penny, but then they could afford it. They were millionaires, having developed and patented several inventions that they sold to industries and then wisely re-invested the proceeds.

It all started when they heard a story about a certain cave in the Kangchenjunga Mountain range in India. That cave appeared to be at the center of several reports of strange occurrences in ancient times of people mysteriously disappearing. The stories had all been handed down by word of mouth until an obscure Spanish scientist and explorer, Jacques LaMande, wrote about it during the 1870s.

Tony and Amanda discovered LaMande's journal in the library of their friend and mentor Dr. Trudy Taylor, who died at the age of ninety-seven and left everything she had to the Steelonni's. She had never married after the love of her life, her husband, died in World War II; they had just been married when he left and they had no children. However, many years later she mentally and emotionally adopted Tony and Amanda and thought of them as her progeny.

Dr. Taylor had studied many branches of science and her library reflected a lifetime of work. It was expansive and invaluable, filling an entire thirty- by twenty-five-foot room, floor to ceiling and overflowing from tables and desks in her home. She had been especially drawn to the metaphysical sciences, focusing on topics beyond physical and human science and delving into the fundamental nature of reality.

She had compiled her collection over a lifetime of studying physics and the natural world. But, while she was a brilliant scientist and teacher, she had been the consummate absent-minded professor and was a horrible organizer, so the collection was scattered and random. It had taken Tony and Amanda months to organize it book-by-book to see exactly what was there. LaMande's journal, as obscure as it was, had gained their immediate attention.

The stories in the old, weather-beaten, leather-bound, four-inch-thick book contained hand-written notes from decades of LaMande's research. The material included many different accounts of explorers who went seeking the cave, then disappeared and were never heard from again. Many of the second- or third-hand stories that managed to make it back mentioned a greenish glow coming from the cave that had drawn explorers in. LaMande had even included a hand-drawn map depicting the cave's possible, approximate location.

LaMande wrote that he went to the mouth of the cave with his most trusted assistant, Pierre Ortagus. However, he wisely gave his journal to Ortagus and instructed him to wait outside the cave and if he didn't return in three days, to leave and tell the world what had happened. Under no circumstances, he ordered Ortagus, was he to follow him into the cave. At the end of the third day when LaMande had not returned, Ortagus did as he was instructed.

However, with little standing in the scientific community and with only the journal as proof, Ortagus was never able to convince fellow scientists that LaMande's disappearance had been anything except a terrible accident. Nobody was willing to organize and fund another expedition to find LaMande.

Ortagus put the journal on a shelf in his personal library, where it collected dust until he died and his children donated the contents of his collection to a Spanish library, where it languished on a shelf in a storage room.

Eventually, during a trip to Spain, Dr. Taylor found the innocuous journal for sale at the library and bought it. When she got home, she put it on one of the tables in her library, intending to study it; however, she died of natural causes three days later.

The Steelonni's delved into the journal, using it to eventually find the cave, which indeed emitted a greenish glow; they were elated, but sad that Dr. Taylor never knew what she had found. They determined that they would eliminate emotion from this discovery and keep their investigation strictly to a scientific approach. Whatever was in that cave had apparently caused the disappearance of quite a few people, so it would call for careful handling.

The cave entrance was hidden, overgrown with shrubs and vines, so it took quite an effort for them and the locals they'd hired to clear it. They instructed their crew to wait outside the cave and if they weren't out in three days, to alert local authorities and mount a rescue effort. Since they'd paid the crew only half their fee, the other half payable at the end of the expedition, the Steelonni's expected they would follow their instructions.

They entered the cave at eight-thirty a.m. and were able to walk quite easily along the eight-foot wide path, with the ceiling arched up a good eight feet above their heads. The tunnel walls and ceiling were unnaturally smooth, not like the jagged walls of other caves they'd explored. The floor was covered in fine dirt that rose in puffs of dust as their boots marched along.

They could see the greenish glow coming from somewhere ahead. After walking about half a mile along the curiously straight path, they emerged into a cavernous rotunda almost perfectly rounded out with no other entrance or exit.

The rotunda was abnormally perfect, as if its rock sides had been laser-cut. It wasn't all that big, maybe thirty feet in diameter, rising to a rounded-out ceiling about ten feet high. The floor was rock so smooth it looked like brushed concrete. In the middle of the rotunda a round, stone pedestal rose about four feet high and three feet in diameter, looking like it had been cut from the rock. In the middle of the pedestal lay a green-glowing piece of jagged rock about the size of a soccer ball.

Not knowing what the material was and not wanting to join the ranks of other missing scientists, Tony and Amanda stopped in their tracks when they saw the glowing material. They looked at each other and Amanda grabbed Tony's hand and with a bright smile said, with her distinctive southern accent derived from her Atlanta, Georgia upbringing, "Darlin', I think we found it!" Her syrup-sweet southern drawl was one of the many things Tony loved about her.

"Yes we did," he replied with an unmistakable Boston inflection, smiling back, "Whatever 'it' is…" he added, his voice trailing off as he studied the dead-end cave. "Does this place look like it was put here by someone other than Mother Nature?"

"Yes, absolutely," she said as she reached out to run her hands over the sides of the rotunda. Tony gently grabbed her sleeve and stopped her before she touched the wall. "Until we have a better idea what we're dealing with I think we should use bio-hazard protocols."

"Hmm, you could be right," Amanda said. "Good idea, let's suit up."

They each retrieved, from their packs, personal protective equipment, or PPE, which included coveralls coated with nonporous protective material, gloves, self-contained filtered respirators, eye protection, boots and hoods with clear face plates. The PPE would help protect them from anything harmful infiltrating through the suit – at least they hoped so.

Suited up, they proceeded first along the entire circumference of the rotunda looking for anything interesting. They found nothing but almost perfect, smooth rock. Upon closer examination using a magnifying glass, Amanda could see tiny, concentric, etched lines about a thirty-second of an inch apart running horizontally from top to bottom around the entire circumference of the rotunda.

"I think this rotunda was cut out of the rock using some sort of laser or something," she theorized. "But I don't know of…I can't even imagine…what kind of equipment could have done this with the degree of perfection we're seeing here."

"I agree," said Tony from a kneeling position as he examined the floor closely with a magnifying glass. "This floor is smooth as a baby's behind and the dust on the floor is actually tiny particles that look like the rock of this cave. It looks like the particulate left from laser etching."

When they completed their perimeter walk they came back to the opening that would take them back out. They hesitated there a moment, considering their next move.

"Well, I guess we're wasting time just standing here," Tony said. "We either need to fish or cut bait."

They stood looking at each other; then their gazes both shifted to the green-glowing object on the pedestal. "Let's go take a look," Tony said, grabbing Amanda's right hand in his left and stepping off towards the pedestal. Amanda resisted, pulling him back a step and stopping him.

"I don't know. I've got a bad feeling about this," she said. "We really don't know what we're dealing with here. Maybe we should just leave."

Tony looked at her a long moment, then said, "Exactly, we don't know what we're dealing with. But, we're scientists, we're explorers, we're inventors. We deal with not knowing quite a bit. We've never let that stop us in the past. We just need to be careful and cautious and approach this like we would any other foreign substance. We'll never know unless we try."

"Yeah, OK, enough said," she admitted, a bit irritated at how logically Tony always approached things. It drove her crazy sometimes. "OK, let's do it," she said, this time grabbing his hand and propelling them both the ten paces to the pedestal.

9

TOUCHING TIME

WHEN TONY AND AMANDA GOT TO the stone column, they stopped about three feet from it and did a 360-degree walk-around before touching anything. The pedestal looked exactly like the walls, smooth and showing the tiny etch marks up the entire structure. The top was polished and smooth like the cave's floor.

Then there was the glowing green substance; actually, as they looked at it more closely, the glow appeared to be pulsing slowly, rhythmically. Unlike the floor and sides of the cave, the green substance was jagged and rough. It looked like a rock of some sort, but it wasn't anything the two scientists could identify.

"It kind of looks like a piece of meteor rock - do you think it's safe to touch it?" Tony asked.

"Hmm, well, as you said, we'll never know unless we try," Amanda said as she reached out her gloved hand and touched the rock. She felt a tingle on her hand, but nothing happened. Her glove, like the rest of her suit, was made from impenetrable, synthetic material that blocked all known biohazardous materials. She looked at Tony and shrugged. "I guess we can touch it with gloves on," she said, smiling at him.

He just shook his head and grinned. She was impetuous and even though she was careful, she was also a risk taker – which sometimes backfired on her, but not this time. "Yep, I guess we can, *thank you*," he said with a slight scolding tone. "So now what?"

"Well, we need to study it back in our lab so we'll need to take it with us, I guess," Amanda said, ending her statement with an upward lilt of her voice, making it a statement and a question too.

"You are right, but it's a risk because we don't know what will happen if we take it from this cave, where it has obviously been placed or somehow got here and has been here for…well, for we don't know how long…," he said. "But…."

"But we're scientist, we're explorers, we're inventors, this is what we do," she said, completing his thought and his sentence, as they often did to each other. After 27 years of marriage, they'd come to appreciate this.

"OK," he said as he reached into his backpack and retrieved a drawstring bag made of the same material as their suits. "Grab it and bag it."

Amanda grinned, reached down and placed both hands under the rock – she definitely felt a tingle in both hands and halfway up her arms - and her vision blurred a little, making the room, Tony, the pedestal, and everything else shimmer like Georgia heat rising off a hot tin roof in the middle of July. She shook her head a little to clear her vision, but it didn't help much. She attempted to hoist the green rock towards the bag…but it wouldn't budge. She got closer to the pedestal to get better footing and leverage and gave another tug. No movement.

"Umm, either I need to get into the gym and hit the free weights or this thing is lots heavier than it looks. It won't move," she said, standing up. Her vision slowly cleared as soon as her hands left the rock.

"Here, let me try," said Tony as he handed her the bag. He did workout almost every day in their home gym, so he was prepared to go macho on her and show her how a man does it. He assumed a weight-lifter's stance, looking like he was about to perform a world-record dead lift. He squatted, put both hand under the rock and immediately let go and jumped back.

"EEEYOWW! HOLEY MOLEY!" he squealed. "Did you feel that tingle?"

"Yes, I did, but it doesn't appear to have done any harm," she said.

"Well, it would have been nice if you'd said something before I touched it," he retorted.

"Well, you went all gung-ho and didn't give me time, dear…and you didn't ask," she shot back pensively, sticking her bottom lip out in a pout she did when her feelings got hurt. "And just so you know, your vision may go funky too."

"OK," he said, never being able to stay mad at her for long, especially when she gave that cute little pout. "I guess I had that coming. Let me give it another try now." He reached down again, assumed the stance, put his hands under the rock and felt the tingle as he pulled upward on the rock, expecting resistance, already mentally placing the rock into the bag in Amanda's outstretched arms, and…nothing happened. The soccer-ball sized rock just sat there like it was part of the pedestal. His vision blurred and the room started shimmering but he kept his grip.

He strained for a few seconds, then gave up, stepped back, let his vision clear, and said, "It's like it's glued or bolted to the pedestal. I don't know how to remove it." As he talked he reached into his pack and retrieved a flat, beveled chisel, which he slid between the rock and the top of the pedestal, trying to pry it up, to no avail.

"Maybe we're going about this the wrong way," Amanda said. "We don't need the whole rock to study it. We just need a small piece. Maybe we can chip off a piece to take back to the lab."

"Excellent idea," Tony replied, reaching into his pack for a 10-ounce hammer. He placed the chisel tip on a jagged piece of the rock and gently tapped the head of the chisel with the hammer. He expected resistance, but to his surprise a fragment about as thick as a quarter, six inches wide and twelve inches long, chipped off and fell with a hard thunk onto the pedestal.

"Um, that was easier than I thought it would be," he said. "Do we have a sample jar we can put that into before we put it in the bag?"

"Yes we do," Amanda said as she shuffled through her pack until she found a fourteen-inch long metal jar that looked like a coffee thermos with a twist-off top. She took the top off and reached to pick up the small fragment. But it was so heavy she had to slide it along the top of the pedestal to slide it into the jar. It hit the bottom with a clang and she nearly dropped it when the weight hit the jar.

"Whoa, that is one heavy substance," she said as she hoisted it back to the pedestal. "You're carrying this thing," she told Tony, sliding the jar into his pack. "The good news is I didn't feel any tingling through the jar."

"Yeah, that tingling and vision thing worries me a little," he said. "Let's get some pictures and get out of here." He took a small digital camera from his pack and walked the perimeter of the rotunda taking pictures of everything. Then he attached the camera to a small tripod, set the timer and got several pictures and some video with both of them at the pedestal with the glowing rock, to document that they were really there.

Then they headed out. It seemed to them that they'd only been at the pedestal for about thirty minutes. But, when they got to the mouth of the cave the sun was dipping below the horizon and their crew was setting up camp for the evening.

Amanda glanced at her watch. She tapped the face of it and said, "Dang, my watch must be wrong. What time do you have?"

"It's…," Tony started to say as he looked at his watch, then stopped and stared at it a moment. He looked up at her and continued, "It's six-thirty p.m. We've been in there for ten hours!"

"We definitely need to study that rock," Amanda said. She recalled Einstein's Theory of Special Relativity. It hypothesized that objects in a strong gravitational field, such as earth, are part of a space-time continuum; and, that when two massive objects exert equal force, a person caught between the gravitational fields can experience time at a different rate than someone outside the field.

She knew that the object in the cave must be very high density, based on its extreme weight. So maybe it was exerting a strong magnetic field in which they were immersed, which might explain why they felt like they were only gone thirty minutes when it was actually ten hours. They were also exhausted. Both of them felt like they'd just run a marathon. They ate what their crew had prepared for supper, then retired to the large tent that had been set up for them. They couldn't resist taking the substance out and examining it, wearing gloves but none of the other protective suit.

After a minute of looking at the substance, Amanda shook her head as if coming out of a trance and asked Tony, "Is your vision blurring really badly?"

"Yeah, and my head is spinning like a top…I think we need to put this away until we can get it back to the lab and examine it under safer controlled conditions."

"Agreed," she said, quickly sliding it into the metal bottle and back into the back pack. "We also don't want to give this crew we hired any idea of what we have here."

Outside the tent, two of the crew huddled at the camp fire, glancing nervously at the tent as they saw it glowing green. "This is a very, very bad thing," said one of the men in Hindi language. He was the crew's leader, Armanio Vargas. "I have heard stories of many who have disappeared looking for an ancient green substance. These people may have found it, but they do not understand it. This can be very dangerous for all of us."

They broke camp early the next morning and began the long trek back to civilization. They eventually arrived at an airport where they paid the crew and boarded a private jet they'd chartered. As they made their way back to Boston, Amanda wondered where the rock in the cave had originated. Who had excavated that perfect tunnel and rotunda, and how, and why? These mysteries might never be solved, but at least now they could study the substance and possibly get some answers.

When they arrived home, Tony and Amanda began testing and experimenting on the substance. They decided to keep their find a secret, even from their son Sam, until they had a better idea of what they actually had. In hindsight, that wasn't a great decision.

However, they did name it so they could stop calling it the "green substance." After careful consideration, they chose Amtonium – intertwining their first names and tagging "ium" on the end, borrowing from the Latin model used in naming metallic elements. They shortened that name in daily use to "Amton."

After weeks of experiments, which they documented in blue notebooks, they determined that beyond a doubt this substance was not of this earth. Where it came from and how it got here was still a mystery, but their theory was that it had extraterrestrial origins and that someone had deliberately concealed it in that cave for unknown reasons.

There was much they didn't understand about Amtonium and they had more questions than answers. However, one thing they did know was that even their small chip exerted an extremely powerful, external force that altered their perspective of time.

They decided to focus on that and after months of work they developed two control devices by dividing the fragment into six pieces, each piece being two-inches wide by six-inches long. They used four pieces to make the two preliminary control devices; each device used two pieces of Amtonium. They placed the remaining two pieces into a titanium case for later use. The case was put into a two-inch thick floor safe that was inside a larger walk-in safe with four-inch steel walls.

The control devices – which they dubbed "TimeCon," short for time controller – were crude, but they enabled them to change the intensity and frequency of the unknown force using high-density shielding. They discovered through experimentation that a one-eighth-inch thick sheet of a new titanium-gold alloy called Ti3Au, placed between the two chips, neutralized the gravitational fields.

When they pressed the green button on the TimeCon, the shielding slid aside enough for the two fields to intersect. They discovered that they could control how far back in time they went by using the digital time dial, which controlled how far the Ti3Au barrier slid open, thus limiting the amount of Amton exposed. The wider the gap, the further back in time they'd go. It wasn't precise, yet, but it worked.

They actually traveled back and forth in time. Their first experiments were conservative and careful, opening the gap millimeters at a time, only going back a few minutes.

Tony was the first to try it. He kissed Amanda, said, "See you in a couple minutes - hopefully," then stepped back about five paces and pushed the green button. Amanda stayed in exactly the same spot as she watched Tony get consumed by a frightening but beautiful whirlwind of light and smoke. He looked at her with a nervous smile, waved and said, "Adios."

"I hope we've done the right thing..." she said to him, but he didn't hear because he'd just vanished. Just as they'd planned, she stayed in the same spot so that when he pushed the red return or "home" button she'd be there. The home button pushed the Ti3Au barrier the exact same distance in the other direction, bringing them back to the point where they'd started – theoretically anyway.

It was the longest two minutes of her life. She was excited by the potential of their discovery but frightened by the consequences of their actions. Just as she was beginning to panic as she realized he may not return, the hair on the back of her neck and her whole head began to lift up from static electricity. She felt a kind of pressure like that exerted by an approaching train in a subway tunnel. Then she saw the sparkling lights and swirling smoke of the time tunnel and a blurry image of Tony in its midst, throwing her a smile and thumbs up.

For Tony, the ride had been exhilarating but entirely too short. He'd been gone two minutes from Amanda's perspective, but for him it was only a few seconds. When he pushed the green button he was engulfed in a beautiful storm cloud that formed a swirling tunnel that got smaller as it disappeared infinitely into the distance. It was amazing; he was standing still but still felt the exhilaration of a high-speed ride. There were flashes of light that looked like lighting, but it passed through him with no impact. There were sparkles of multi-colored light cascading down that looked like glitter permeating the tunnel.

In a few seconds the spinning tunnel began to slow down and the smoky mist began to clear. As it did, Tony gasped as he saw before him – well, he saw himself and Amanda. They were in the lab looking at him with wide eyes and dropped jaws.

He had gone back about two minutes and what he saw was he and Amanda preparing to send him back in time. It made sense. That's where he was two minutes ago. But he didn't remember seeing himself two minutes ago; but then, he wouldn't because he had already left…

"Oh, this is going to be tricky to get used to," he thought, as he hit the red return button, hoping it would reverse the process and take him home.

The reverse ride was equally exciting and, as hoped, as the mist cleared and the spinning tunnel dissipated, Tony was greeted by a big hug and a soft kiss from Amanda.

"Oh honey I am so glad to see you," she said in her sweet southern style. "Did it work?"

"Oh yeah, it worked," he gasped. "I went back and saw us looking at me, but I guess neither of us would remember that since we are in the present, not the past. OK, I'm a bit muddled on that point. I guess the you-and-me of two minutes ago still exist, but on a different plane of existence. For the few seconds that I was there both "me's" existed at the same time. I'm not sure what would have happened if I'd stayed. Would one of us have just disappeared? Or would we both exist in the same time?"

"One of you is more than enough at one time. I don't think the world is ready for two of you," Amanda said, joking, but with a hint of sincerity. "I think there's going to be a steep learning curve with this time travel."

"Yes, we're definitely writing the manual on it," he replied. "Let's document this and continue with the experiments." Amanda was already writing in a blue notebook.

In the following months they kept extending the time they went back, first minutes, then hours, then weeks, then months at a time. They alternated trips between the two of them, always leaving one behind as a precautionary measure; but then they began to get impatient. They wanted to find out how powerful this substance was.

So one day Tony picked up one of the controllers and said to Amanda, "Let's see how far back we can go. Have you ever wanted to see the Colosseum in ancient Rome?" He already knew the answer because she obsessed about the Roman civilization.

"Absolutely," said Amanda, who was holding the other controller. She was always up for an adventure and had begun to get uncharacteristically impetuous, as had Tony. They were departing from a pure scientific approach to more of an explorer's attitude. They would find out later that radiant energy from Amton was affecting their brain and causing this impulsive attitude.

"OK, let's try for AD 80," Tony said, dialing it into his controller. He picked that date because he knew that was the year the Colosseum was opened. The words were barely out of his mouth when Amanda dialed that date into her controller, grabbed his hand and hit the green send button. As she jerked him towards her, he lost the grip on his controller and it fell to the workbench with a thump that nobody heard. Tony and Amanda were already gone in a blaze of flashing lights and puffs of iridescent blue smoke that swirled and sparkled, then got slurped into thin air.

Much to their joy and amazement, and chagrin, they found themselves in what looked like the eye of a tornado; there were flashes of what appeared to be lighting though there was no smell of ozone. They felt accelerated movement but weren't moving their legs. They weren't being buffeted around; in fact, it was a pretty smooth ride.

"Tony, what are we doing?" Amanda asked with a mixture of excitement, fear, and confusion in her voice. They hadn't experienced this phenomenon in their previous, much, much shorter time jumps. They had taken a giant leap backwards; like a baby going from crawling to sprinting in a day's time. "I think we may have jumped the gun a little, no, a lot, maybe departed from the empirical method of scientific discovery."

Tony was also having mixed feelings, but he quickly decided they were committed so they may as well enjoy it and learn from the experience – if they survived it. "Well, on the bright side, we are still alive and talking and holding hands," he said, giving her hand a hard squeeze.

After what seemed like five minutes, the spinning slowed down, the colorful light flashes subsided, the smoke cleared, and they were able to see snippets of activity outside the time tunnel. They saw buildings and people dressed in homespun garments, some draped with robes, some with sandals, some barefoot.

Then the tunnel stopped and began to dissipate, clearing their field of vision. They could see that they had been transported to an alleyway in what looked to them like ancient Rome. They gave each other blank stares and both realized at the same time that they hadn't really thought this through.

"Oops, I think we succeeded," said Tony, seeing that Amanda was dressed in a rough, cloth dress of a Roman middle-class woman; looking down he saw that his clothes were the male equivalent. "Maybe this wasn't such a great idea."

10

TAKE A NOTE

Sam and Cici stood at the foot of the basement stairs at Sam's house, ready to launch a search for scientific research notes that might provide a clue to help them find Sam's parents.

"Don't your parents usually keep their notes in those composition books?" Cici asked. Sam appreciated that she knew almost as much about his parents as he did.

"Yep, different colors for different experiments," he replied. "In this case, since this is associated with the field of metaphysics, I'd guess blue."

With a nod Cici strode forward saying, "OK, blue it is, let's start looking...blue notebooks, blue notebooks," as she flipped papers over and picked through boxes.

After several minutes of shuffling through various stacks of papers, maps, reference books and miscellaneous items, Sam shouted, "Eureka, I think I found it!"

Cici saw Sam holding a blue Marble Composition book...actually, three of them rubber-banded together. On the cover in a blank space left for identifying contents, were two words that told them they'd found the right books; *Time Travel*.

"Did you know that your parents were experimenting with time travel?" she asked Sam, arching one eyebrow up questioningly.

"Well, yes...and no...I knew they were interested in it and I know they were studying it but I had no idea they were actually doing experiments," he said, a bit embarrassed that this had slipped by him.

"Hmmm, it would have been nice if they'd confided in you, but these books should give us some clues."

The two sat down on the floor as Sam removed the rubber bands, which is when he saw an old, leather journal that was smaller than the composition books jammed between its three larger companions. Written in cursive, faded black ink on the front cover was the title, *Scientific Journal of Jacques LaMande.*

"Jacques LaMande…that name sounds familiar," Sam shared with Cici. "I've heard my parents talk about him. He was a Spanish scientist in the late 1800's, but I have no idea what he did."

The composition books were numbered one, two and three. "Let's start from the beginning," Cici said as she pulled number one from Sam's pile and opened to the first page. Sam read over her shoulder where he saw in precise flowing handwriting that must be his mother's, the opening statement, "The following information constitutes the research, experiments and findings of Doctors Tony and Amanda Steelonni in regards to the theory and reality of time travel."

"Wow, sounds like they were pretty deep into it," he said absently.

"Well, duh," Cici said with a grin.

For the next four hours they scoured all three notebooks and Dr. LaMande's journal to try and fully understand how his parents had disappeared and where to start looking for them. The last entry was just two days ago.

"OK, so we now know they found a mysterious, extremely dense, green glowing substance they call Amtonium. They think it is extraterrestrial and figured out how to harness its power to travel in time," Cici summarized. Sam was amazed at how she could take a completely complicated subject and break it down to its basic elements.

"Correct," he confirmed. "However, I postulate that they went too far back in time and perhaps the substance lacks the power for the return trip."

Neither Sam nor Cici claimed to be experts or even knowledgeable novices in time travel. It was a very complicated subject and one that took most people longer than they'd been alive to even begin to comprehend. They knew that Einstein's Theory of Special Relativity allowed for the possibility of "wormholes," which are tunnels through space-time that connect distant parts of the universe, and possibly intersect different time dimensions.

However, if the "mouths" of a wormhole move relative to one another, then traversing the bridge between different points in space-time may have taken Sam's parents to a different geographic point in time from where they started. In other words, they weren't in Boston anymore.

"This is giving me a headache," Sam moaned. "We are not going to unravel the mysteries of time travel! My mom and dad may be in serious trouble and may never get back!" he said, a note of desperation in his voice.

"Sam, take a few deep breaths, count to ten and relax a minute," Cici said, echoing her father's often-repeated advice. "For your parents' sake we have to prioritize our plan to the most important issues. Let's not worry about the theory, let's focus on the facts and get them back."

Cici's calm voice and sage words sank in. Sam closed his eyes, breathed deeply and exhaled slowly, counting to ten as he did it. "What would I do without you," he said to her after two or three more breaths.

"You'd be lost in space-time," she said with a giggle. "What, too soon?" she added when she saw the look of shock her flippant joke brought to his face. They locked eyes and something special passed between them, causing them to both burst out laughing.

"OK, I needed that," Sam said as he got his chuckling under control. "Laughter is the best medicine. Now, let's come up with a plan. We know that this remote control device, the time controller or TimeCon - works because I've gone back in time twice and got home. The TimeCon was set on AD 80 when I found it, so that's probably where my parents are, I hope. We know I went from AD 80 to 1775 and then hit the "Home" button and got back here."

"So if you did it why can't your parents do the same thing?" Cici asked pointedly, playing devil's advocate. Then, answering her own question, "I'll tell you why – because the chip of mysterious substance they brought back with them isn't powerful enough to bring both of them all the way back and they haven't figured out that they can possibly come back in steps, hopping from one time to another."

"That sounds logical," Sam said, "But if you're right then we have no idea where they are or why they haven't made it back yet. Something terrible could have happened along the way, or maybe they got separated in time from each other…"

"Stop!" Cici said, not loudly, but sharply enough to stop Sam in mid-sentence with his mouth opened to say his next word. "We can't help them by panicking. We've got to stay calm and systematic about this. We could also use some help. I think we should get my parents involved."

"Eventually, but for their own good, not until we know more about it. My parents were keeping this a secret for a reason," Sam surmised. "They've made a few of their colleagues jealous or even angry with them along the way, beating some of them to inventions. This kept others from making the money they've made so we don't know who we can trust, and I don't want to put your parents in danger. There was one guy, Dr. Ivan Molnikov, who was especially aggressive trying to top them, but he always seemed to come up a day late and a dollar short."

"So we're on our own. It's up to us to find them and get them home," Cici said in a matter-of-fact voice and a shrug of her shoulders, like she was talking about going down to the corner store for a loaf of bread. "Piece o' cake."

"Well, if we assume they went back to AD 80 then that would be the logical place to start looking," Sam said, catching her gung-ho attitude. "I know my mother was obsessed with ancient Rome and she always talked about the great Colosseum there. If I had to guess, that's where I'd start looking."

"OK, so we're going back to ancient Rome," Cici said, her voice exuding her enthusiasm. In spite of the inherent danger, she liked the challenge of the unknown and adventure. "Now, let's figure out how we can do that smartly and safely – and hopefully without running into any lions, or tigers, or bears."

11

MOLNIKOV'S REVENGE

As Sam and Cici began developing their plan, Dr. Ivan Molnikov was coming up with a plan of his own; a plan to end the incessant meddling of Tony and Amanda Steelonni once and for all…and it didn't matter how.

The Russian physicist had been destined to be conflicted from birth. His first name, Ivan, meant "God's grace." However, he never felt as though God, or mortals for that matter, liked him much; in fact, most people considered him arrogant, rude and overbearing. Some people even considered him evil.

Molnikov may have once been a good-looking man, with a square jaw, rugged features and narrow, hazel eyes. However, years of deceit, distrust and double-dealing had left him ragged and bitter.

He had a scraggly, gray beard, not because he liked beards, but because he hated shaving. Some men look good in beards; Molnikov wasn't one of them. It made him look even more sinister, like he was hiding something behind that uneven layer of bristle that transitioned into long, oily hair pulled back in a ponytail because it was easier than washing and combing it. At five-feet, ten-inches tall and 265 pounds he was about eighty pounds overweight and so he sweat too much because everything was an effort.

His parents were political dissidents who had met when they were imprisoned in a gulag, a forced-labor camp, in Siberia.

They conceived him there, brought him into this world and then both died in the prison camp, leaving him to be raised by foster families, the state and when he turned fifteen, by himself. He never forgave his parents for delivering him into such a disrupted life.

He worked on farms, in the city and anywhere he could get room and board until he finagled his way at age eighteen onto a whaling ship, which gave him a glimpse into the wider world that existed outside Russia.

He was a stout man in his youth, strong, barrel-chested, and he was a brawler. He learned to beat older, more experienced fighters with quickness and agility. He was a survivor.

When he turned 20, he bought passage to the United States and ended up in Boston. He was a highly intelligent and driven man who worked his way through college and post-graduate school and earned his doctorate in physics. He yearned to distinguish himself in his field, but time after time just as he was about to make a breakthrough discovery, Tony and Amanda Steelonni would make it first.

They were doing it again. He was on the brink of finding a mysterious substance rumored to affect the time-space continuum, when he heard through his back channels that they may have already found it. Rumor had it that they'd found a journal that led them to the substance.

"Ivan, the Steelonni's just returned from an expedition to India and I've heard they brought back a package that they are not talking about," Molnikov's paid informant in India, Rishabh, had told him over the phone in his sing-song Indian accent that drove the Russian crazy; but his information was normally good.

"You fool, that doesn't help me much. What was in the package!" Molnikov barked at Rishabh, who disliked his employer but liked his money.

"They were very protective of their secret, but I have eyes and ears everywhere, so it is possible that with a bit more persuasion I could get you more information," the informant said, infuriating Molnikov. "By persuasion I assume you mean more money, you cur!" spat Molnikov in a heavy, Russian accent, wishing his informant was in front of him so he could wring his neck. "I have paid you well and you haven't given me anything yet. Tell me what you know and I will decide if you deserve more money!"

"I have talked with some of the men hired by the Steelonni's," said Rishabh, sensing that he was pushing his luck with the volatile Russian. "They said that the Steelonni's found a cave that was glowing green and wouldn't let them go inside with them. They said they were gone for more than ten hours and when they returned they thought they'd only been gone for thirty minutes – and they had something in a specimen canister that they were keeping wrapped up in their pack."

"Now you have earned what I've already paid you," Molnikov said more calmly. "If you want more, you have to give me more."

"Oh, I haven't gotten to the good part yet," said Rishabh, smiling into the phone, knowing that he was playing the Russian like a Stradivarius violin. He'd kept the juiciest information until last, knowing he could squeeze a little more money out of his employer.

"Yes, you see, I talked with two of the men on the expedition, one of them the head guide. They confirmed that during one of their overnight stops they observed the Steelonni's going into their pack to retrieve a specimen jar. When they took the lid off, it glowed green…"

Rishabh stopped, letting that sink into the Russian's thick skull, knowing he had harpooned him like Molnikov used to harpoon whales. "You say it glowed green?" Molnikov said with a bit of a whine in his voice. "Did they actually see what it was?"

"Well, not up close; from a distance it looked like a small piece of rock, but whatever it was they said it was the source of the green glow," Rishabh said slowly, dropping the last little bombshell of information.

"It glowed green – and it seemed to make the Steelonni's – well, here it gets a bit fuzzy, but it seemed to make them fade out and then, they just, disappeared for a while."

That was it, that was all he had, but Rishabh knew it was enough. He was sure there was much more to this story, but he'd given Molnikov enough to earn some extra cash.

"Hmmm, fade and then disappear," Molnikov said suspiciously. "Were your informants perhaps under the influence of drugs? It sounds like they were sampling local loco weed. Disappear, hah! Do you take me for a fool? I am not paying you for such preposterous information!"

Molnikov knew it actually wasn't that preposterous. If the substance was what he'd heard about in his research, it could be that the informants had actually witnessed a distortion in the space-time field. But he didn't want Rishabh to get over-confident.

"I tell you what, I will send you an extra two thousand U.S. dollars for this feeble report and be done with you," the Russian said with finality. "You call me if you hear anything else, but it better be important information next time." Then he hung up the phone.

Next time…time, indeed, was the issue here. He had heard a story –a myth really - about a substance supposedly brought to earth by extraterrestrials tens of thousands of years ago, long before man existed, and hidden in a cave somewhere. India was one of the places it was whispered to be.

The substance was thought to have qualities that somehow broke through barriers of time and space. The legends suggested that this group of aliens hid it to keep it out of the hands of others on their planet because they believed that time travel was dangerous and wrong. They reasoned that it would never be found on this uninhabited, backwater little planet.

Perhaps they were right, thought Molnikov. If the more advanced alien race thought it was dangerous, perhaps humans should leave well enough alone. But humans are a curious species - and greedy.

Discovering a means to travel through time would make the discoverer famous, rich and powerful.

Molnikov wanted that; it appeared the Steelonni's had found it. So it was that Molnikov began to plan how he was going to get it from them.

12

A GLIMPSE OF SAM

Tony and Amanda knew they couldn't stay in the alleyway forever; they were just lucky they'd accidently transported themselves to a secluded place where they could collect their thoughts and figure out what to do next.

Obviously, something had gone right because they'd done it, they'd gone back to the year AD 80; but it also had gone terribly wrong. They both were not supposed to be here; they had agreed that when they were ready to really test their time travel theories one of them would go, so that the other could be in a position to help if things went wrong – which they certainly had.

They had pressed the red "Home" button on their TimeCon, but nothing had happened. It may have been because the remote he had dropped at the lab was also set to 80 A.D. and that kept their remote from working. However, it was also possible that the Amtonium lacked potency to fuel two people doing back-to-back time jumps spanning nearly 2,000 years.

Either way, whether they'd made a mistake in their calculations, in making the device, or it was just an unintended consequence, they were stranded in time.

"I love you dearly and you know I'd go anywhere with you, so don't take this the wrong way, but why are you here?" Tony said to Amanda.

"I could ask you the same thing," she shot back at him with a perplexed and worried look in her clear, blue eyes. "I was supposed to be the one who came back to ancient Rome, not you." Then she remembered that she had actually grabbed his hand and hit the green button, so she stopped talking and furrowed her brow.

Tony hated seeing her worry, so he eased up a bit. He intentionally waited a few seconds and smiled when he answered, "Well, the good news is we're both alive and transported here apparently with all our parts where they should be. Oh, and I must tell you that you are even more fetching and beautiful dressed as an ancient Roman maiden."

He gave her a deliberate head-to-toe and back again once over, then tilting his head forward, twitched his dark eyebrows up and down a couple times and gave her a sideways grin she could never resist; after twenty seven years of marriage it still sent chills up her spine when he did that.

Amanda couldn't help but giggle and blush as she looked down at her clothing and responded, "*Es vir pulcher*" which translated from Latin to, "You are a very handsome man." She spoke passable Latin, which could prove helpful in their current situation, since that was the language used in ancient Rome.

"*Grazie bella signora*," replied Tony, this time in Italian, with a wink and smile as he lifted her hand and kissed it softly. Italian language was rooted in Latin. The couple shared Italian heritage that went back for generations, so looking the part wasn't going to be a problem. Amanda with her fiery, curly auburn hair, blue eyes, and olive complexion reflected her roots in northern Italy while Tony's dark hair, dark skin, and deep brown eyes harkened back to his Sicilian heritage.

"So what do we do next?" Tony asked as he checked in all directions to make sure they weren't drawing undue attention. However, they apparently just looked like two middle-aged lovers making out in an alley. Nobody gave them a second glance.

"Well, when in Rome, do as the Romans do," Amanda responded, drawing a groan from her husband as she used the trite cliché. "Sorry, had to do it," she added.

"Well, right now I suspect we are near the Colosseum," he said, cupping his right hand to his right ear, hearing the roar of a very large and enthusiastic crowd of people several blocks away from their alley. "Since we're both here, why don't we take in a show?"

"Ooh, I like the way you think," Amanda answered, flipping her head, sending her red curls in all directions and getting a devil-may-care attitude in her voice.

This reckless attitude they both seemed to have was totally not like them. Being scientists, they tended to be deliberate and thoughtful about everything they did. It was no coincidence that this new boldness emerged when they started experimenting on the Amtonium. They would learn that it was one of the many inexplicable side effects that would come from close proximity to it.

As she flipped her curls she grabbed her partner's hand and assertively stepped into the busy street. She did this with such force that she didn't notice the clasp break on her charm bracelet, a bracelet she always wore because Sam had given it to her for her birthday. The bracelet fell to the ground behind the stack of baskets.

They were swept up in a sea of human foot traffic flowing towards the sound of the crowd in the amphitheater.

First Century Rome, during the rule of Julius Ceasar, was the world's first multicultural metropolis with a population of more than one million people. However, Rome could not yet handle its own size and status. Like modern large cities today, it had areas of splendor and others of squalor. There were very rich people and more very poor people. It was a dangerous place, and the backstreets were to be avoided after dark or risk being mugged, robbed or worse by groups of thugs.

Fortunately, Amanda was an authority on all things ancient Rome. She had studied the geo-political history and culture of the era. She was more attuned to the time than even the notorious Julius Caesar, the aristocratic general and politician who she knew had just returned from Spain and would soon be elected Consul, the highest office in the republic. Not long after that he would ally himself with fellow military and political leaders Pompey and Crassus to form the powerful "First Triumvirate."

As she guided her husband along the wide street leading to the Colosseum, she could not help but be excited to be on this adventure. She knew they were in uncharted territory. They'd sent themselves back in time and their return home button hadn't worked.

They were stranded in a foreign and dangerous place. She should be frightened; and yet, she was aching to see the Colosseum in its glory. She knew that this was the year Emperor Titus had opened the new Colosseum with a festival that included 100 days of games with gladiators and wild animals.

"You know, the Colosseum is believed to have drinking fountains and latrines," she said to Tony. He was accustomed to her bringing him into her stream of thoughts without any reference point to exactly what she'd been thinking previous to that, so he went with it.

"No, I didn't know that," he said, sure that he would catch up to her constantly-churning thought process soon. "You will be able to now confirm or deny that little historical tidbit."

"Yes, and historians say that wild lions were brought in with the gladiators to add to the danger and drama of the shows," she said, continuing to pull him through the crowd like she'd grown up here instead of popping in from the future.

They turned a corner and were blasted by the crescendo of the Colosseum crowd going wild at something that had happened. It made them both want to get in and see what was going on.

"Um, I'm sure you have an answer to this, but can you share with me exactly how you plan to get us into this place?" Tony asked. He was assuming they'd need tickets or some form of access pass.

"That's easy," she said as she yanked him hard left through one of the seventy-six arched public passageways that led into the belly of the largest amphitheater in the Roman world at that time. "You see, Emperor Titus was well-loved by his people and he wanted to ensure that the Colosseum was a success, so he allowed free access during the 100-day festival."

Impressed with his wife's historical acumen, he just shook his head and let her lead the way. As they emerged from the arched tunnel, a set of steps led up and into the arena. The sound of the crowd roaring was deafening. They stepped into the sunlight to behold a sight that no modern man or woman had ever beheld – the Colosseum in its full glory.

"Geez, this is absolutely amazing," he said to Amanda. She was transfixed, her mind being blown by the fact that she was looking at the complete Colosseum – not the skeletal remains of it after centuries of use, damage from natural elements such as lightening and earthquakes, disrepair from neglect and 400 years of tearing it apart as a source of building materials for other projects.

Tears welled up in her eyes as she saw what it had been, knowing what it would look like in the future. However, she didn't have much time to ponder it. The 50,000 spectators were packed in like sardines and hundreds more were jockeying for a good viewing position, so standing still in the middle of a walkway was dangerous.

"We'd better move it along or we'll draw undue attention," Tony whispered in her ear as he gently grabbed her elbow and guided her up the ramp that led to the spectator seating. They moved along until he spied a space on the concrete, marble-covered seats and pulled her down a bit too abruptly.

"Ouch!" she squealed, "These seats are as hard as...well, hard as a rock." Several heads of spectators nearest them turned when she spoke the words in English.

Tony said to her in a low tone, "You'd better speak Latin sweetie or you'll get us busted."

She glanced around and nodded, whispering, "Oops, sorry, you're right."

Conversation ceased when, at that moment, the entire crowd rose to their feet and began yelling things in Latin such as "occidere eum," which means kill him, or "parcat ei," spare him. These utterances were accompanied by people giving a "thumbs up" or "thumbs down" gesture.

Amanda quietly said to Tony, "You know, the thumbs up or down had opposite meanings in ancient Rome from what they are today and scholars still argue about exact meanings. You'd think thumbs down meant to take the gladiator's life, but many scholars believe that in ancient Rome it actually meant swords down, so the gladiator would live to fight another day. Thumbs up may have meant to thrust a sword up the heart and kill the losing gladiator. Then there are those who believe that to spare a life you hid your thumb inside your fist..."

Normally, Tony would have been very impressed with Amanda's wealth of information, but his attention was drawn to the floor of the amphitheater, where the action was causing the crowd to go crazy.

Amanda and Tony had fortuitously found two good seats, right in the front row on the second tier of seating. Directly in front of them and across the diameter of the amphitheater, Tony saw a gladiator with his back to the wall and two lions circling him, sizing him up. The crowd was deciding the fate of this man.

But what got Tony's attention was the small feline that stood in front of the gladiator, facing off against the two larger lions. The cat was unmistakable. There was only one cat like it in the world. He leaned forward and took a closer look at the gladiator.

Amanda had started to pontificate about another aspect of ancient Roman death games when Tony grabbed her arm and whispered in a raspy voice, "Sweetie, take a look at that gladiator and tell me what you think."

"How rude," Amanda protested, not liking to be interrupted when she was on a roll. However, as she prepared to pout she also did as he asked and in a moment her attitude changed. Her eyes widened and she gasped.

"Well butter my butt and call me a biscuit, is that who I think it is?" she exclaimed, the southern adage coming out due to the stress of the moment. "It can't be him, can it?"

"Look at the cat in front of him and tell me that isn't Raven," Tony suggested, also speaking English because by now the crowd didn't care; they were hungry for blood.

Amanda shifted her gaze to the smaller cat in front of the much larger lions and saw the smaller cat bristle up to look much bigger and fiercer. Even at this distance she recognized the blazing blue eyes; and she recognized the shape of her son even if he was dressed like a Roman gladiator.

"Sweet Jesus, that's Sam!" she cried, as the crowd's lust for blood boiled over and turned them into raving maniacs. "They're going to kill my boy!"

Just as she said this and the lions crouched for their attack, the gladiator, cat, and dog were engulfed in a swirling tornado of dust and smoke and flashes of light. In seconds he was no longer visible. As the dust settled the lions sat down, licked their chops, and stared blankly at the empty space where their prey had been. The crowd murmured in amazement and confusion and Sam's parents breathed a collective sigh of relief.

"Sam found the other remote!" Tony said to Amanda, in English, quietly. "But he doesn't know how to use it and he could end up lost in time like we are! We have got to get the heck out of here and get back home."

With that, he took Amanda's hand and guided her down the steps leading out of the Colosseum and back to their secluded alleyway. "Our home button isn't working but that doesn't mean we can't get back there somehow," he said, desperate to save his son. He dialed in a new date on the remote, grabbed Amanda's hand, and hit the send button.

In a hail of smoke, flashing lights and a whirlwind, they disappeared.

13

TIME TO PLAN

As Tony and Amanda left AD 80 for another time zone, Sam and Cici were in the living room of Sam's house, finalizing plans to go from the present day back to AD 80 as a starting point to find his parents.

"This time, I'd prefer not to land in front of hungry lions or gladiators who are in a kill-or-be-killed state of mind," Sam reasoned. He was stretched out on the over-stuffed sofa, one leg hooked over the back, one arm behind his head and the other hanging down as he reached into an opened bag of salty potato chips.

Akamaru sat patiently nearby, watching Sam's hand full of chips move from the bag to his mouth. The dog's mouth watered and he drooled as he watched, but he was too proud to beg. He waited, knowing his time would come.

Raven was in his familiar spot, stretched along the back of the sofa, not even the least bit interested in the chips, which were not his thing. Now if it was extra-crunchy Cheetos, then he'd be all over it. Lily-Rose sat next to Cici, ambivalent to eating because she wasn't programmed for it, but curious as she saw the dog's apparent fixation on it.

"Any thoughts on how you will avoid lions and gladiators?" Cici asked, with just a hint of skepticism in her voice as she sat in a chair, her arms folded and one leg crossed over the other, peering at Sam like a psychiatrist studying a patient.

"Well, remembering that I'm making this up as I go along, just hear me out before you shoot holes in my plan," Sam replied, crunching on his chips and just a little bit irritated at her cynicism. One of the things Sam liked about Cici is that she often challenged his ideas, which made him slow his roll instead of charging off in the wrong direction; but it did bug him sometimes.

"I've been thinking about it and I think I know where I went wrong last time," he continued. "I am assuming my parents are alive and well somewhere so I'm also assuming that wherever they landed was safe. So, if I – make that, if *we* - could get to the same place we might be able to find a clue to their whereabouts."

"Where were you when you first hit the send button on that remote," Cici asked him, starting to catch his train of thought.

"I was in the basement of the BIT lab," he said. "Why?"

"I'm not sure yet...where did you find the remote?" she queried, starting to treat this conversation like an interrogation.

"I found it in my parents' lab in the basement of our house," he said, beginning to see where she was going with her questioning.

"Was AD 80 dialed in when you found it?" she persisted.

"Yes, yes, yes," Sam interjected as he swung his leg off the back of the couch and flipped himself into a sitting position all in one motion, sending the chips flying as he knocked over the bag.

Akamaru was on it like a large, furry vacuum cleaner, slurping up the stray chips in two sweeps as his drool slung from side to side. Raven peered down at him a bit disdainfully, thinking to himself, "Disgusting – I can see I'll need to give this canine some lessons on eating etiquette." Lily-Rose looked on with academic curiosity about this eating thing.

"Since I found the remote in the home lab, that's where we need to be when we hit the send button...it should get us back to the same place they were..." he trailed off as he started thinking about the science behind his words. He didn't need Cici to start shooting holes in his theory; he was already doing it.

He thought about Albert Einstein's theory. It suggested that the elements of space and time merge together into a space-time continuum that curves in the presence of immense mass, such as the force of gravitational pull. The theory allowed for the possibility of wormholes which were essentially time tunnels that moved through space-time, allowing for the possibility of movement through time.

"The problem is, these wormholes might be constantly moving, so there's no guarantee that we'll land in the same place as they did," he reasoned, knowing that Cici had probably already figured that out as well.

"True, but then again, maybe we will," she said with a hopeful lifting of her voice. "It is theoretically possible that the wormhole didn't move. I mean, we have at least a fifty-fifty chance."

"Well, if it means finding my parents, those are pretty good odds," he said, jumping to his feet, knocking a few more chips to the ground for the vacuum dog to inhale. "That's right boy, we'd better eat up because where we're going eating may not be an option."

As Sam rose Raven rose with him. The cat was not about to leave his friend's side again. He didn't understand exactly what they were about to do, but he fathomed that it was potentially dangerous. So, he needed to try and keep Sam safe, which seemed to be getting harder and harder to do these days.

"So, what do we need to bring along with us?" Cici asked, thinking they should have basics like food, water, extra clothes, flashlights... stuff they might need.

"Well, I don't claim to be an expert on this yet, but I'm not sure bringing things will do us any good, at least based on my two trips," he said. "Both times I got where I was going dressed in period clothing and equipment...though now that you mention it I remember that my watch was still on my wrist. I think for the most part we'll have to find what we need once we get there."

Cici raised her hand like she was in school asking the teacher a question. "I hate to put a fly in the ointment but if we're both going… well, going back in time and hopefully to a safe space…shouldn't we let somebody here know what we're doing so if we get in trouble we have some back up?"

Sam thought about that a moment. If they got in trouble there wasn't really much that anybody in the twenty-first century could do to help. Since there were only two of the controllers, the TimeCons, one with his parents and the other with them, there wasn't a rescue plan; it would be up to them to pull their butts out of the fire. Still, it would be good to at least have someone here who knew what they were doing and why they were missing.

"My parents were being pretty secretive about this project so I don't think they'd want many people to know about it; so who do you think we can trust to bring in on this and keep quiet about it," Sam asked. "Got anybody in mind?"

"First name that comes to me is Charger," said Cici without hesitation.

"That is exactly who I was thinking of too," Sam said. "If we can't trust Charger, who can we trust?"

Charger was one of their closest friends, who they trusted as much as they trusted each other. Charger's real name was Michael C. Banyan, but to his closest friends he was known as Charger – and he liked that.

Charger had an illness in early childhood that had confined him to a wheelchair; however, he never considered that a handicap. Since he grew up with it he had learned how to use the specially-designed racing chair to his advantage. He developed incredible upper body strength from this, which he augmented with exercise, weight lifting and wheelchair basketball.

In fact, the wheelchair led to his nickname "Charger" because from an early age he could blast off in that wheelchair and beat almost anybody in a race. Foot racers might beat him in the first few yards of a race, but once he got the chair going, it was all over for them.

Charger was also a science nerd, very intelligent, adaptable, and resourceful; and, he had an infectious sense of humor so he was always fun to hang out with. They'd all been friends since kindergarten. Sam and Cici knew they could count on Charger to watch their backs.

"OK, I'll give him a call right now," said Sam as he reached for his cell phone. He punched the contacts icon and found Charger's name, which was accompanied by his photo. It showed a nice shot of his handsome face and curly, dark hair. Sam tapped the number and the phone rang.

Charger picked up on the second ring. "Hey Sam, what's happening? This must be important because you rarely call…you just come over and knock on the door." Charger lived right across the street from Sam's house.

"Charger, very perceptive and very right, this is a life and death call!" Sam said, knowing that would get Charger's attention. Normally there would have been at least a minute of small talk and friendly barbs before anything serious was discussed. When Sam said "life and death" Charger immediately sat up straighter in his chair, his bluish-green eyes widening as he pulled the phone closer to his ear.

"Oh, this doesn't sound good…what the heck is going on?" he asked.

"My parents are missing. I think they have gotten lost in time, so Cici and I are going back in time and try to find them. We need you to come over to my house and be our home base and get us back if we get in trouble," Sam blurted, trying to summarize the myriad events he'd experienced in the last couple days.

"OK, I pretty much stopped listening after you said your parents are lost in time, but hold tight, I'll be over there in a jiffy," Charger said, hanging up. Less than two minutes later he was bursting through the front door, not bothering to knock.

"So, slow down and start from the beginning, tell me what happened," he said, coming to a skidding halt in front of Sam. For several minutes Sam and Cici explained the situation and answered

Charger's questions, of which he had plenty, as usual. Charger was a very meticulous interviewer, wanting to make sure he understood what was being said.

"Wow," was all he could say for a moment after the explanation brought him up to the present. "Wow that is like drinking from a firehose…lots of incredible information. If it was anybody but you two telling me this I'd be calling the men in the white jackets to pick you up and take you to your happy place."

Sam and Cici couldn't help but laugh as Charger screwed up his face, placed the fingertips of both hands on his forehead and then splayed them outward, uttering a "pchuu" sound to simulate his exploding head.

"When exactly do you intend to go on this suicide mission," he asked, trying to keep his voice calm even as his mind wasn't. "I mean, really, you guys are talking about literally going into the lion's den with no weapons and nothing but the clothes on your back – clothes which will change once you get wherever you're going – and then not knowing if you can find your parents or even if you can actually come back, at least not to this dimension. I mean, I gotta' tell you, it sounds like a really bad idea."

"Well, when you put it that way it does sound a bit crazy," Sam said. "And I admit it's probably not the smartest thing we've ever done, but I don't see any alternatives. If you've got any ideas, I'm all ears…"

Hearing none, Sam continued. "In answer to your question, we are going to leave immediately because time is of the essence, pun intended. So let's go," he said as he led the way to the freight elevator that they used to get Charger to the basement. Along the way they discussed what Charger would do in case they didn't return in three days.

When they had all assembled in front of the work bench in the lab, Sam turned to Raven and Akamaru and said, "I think you two should stay here with Charger, just in case things don't work out."

Raven jumped to Sam's side and pressed against his left leg, saying, "No way boss, where you go, I go. Somebody's got to keep you out of trouble."

Akamaru slowly walked over to Sam's right side, turned and sat down. "I've seen you two in action," he said to Sam and Raven. "Somebody's got to keep you both out of trouble. Don't get me wrong, I'm not too crazy about getting my cells all scrambled up with the possibility of getting some nasty cat genes transferred in the process," he said, giving one of his crooked dog grins that really looked like a scowl.

Of course, Charger and Cici only heard wuffs and barks but Raven and Sam understood. Sam told the other two humans what the animals had said, demonstrating his ability to understand them.

"You guys go ahead, I'll be OK," Charger asserted, putting on his bravest face. "You need more help wherever you're going than I need it here Sam."

Cici interjected, "Uh, excuse me, but our little Lily-Rose can provide more than adequate security. She can zap several thousand volts from her nose and I'm not even getting into what can come out the other end." Lily-Rose sent a crackling bolt of electricity between her nostrils, just to emphasize the point. "She's smart too – like super-computer smart."

"Cici is right," Sam said. "Charger, there may be some bad folks who would like to get their hands on these notes or the green rock. You'll need Akamaru here. He is an awesome dude. Oh, I think it would be a good idea if you came with me on a short time jump with Akamaru so that you can understand him. It'll make it much easier on both of you."

"Really, you can understand him?" Charger asked. Then his eyes widened and his voice rose as he realized what Sam had just said. "Wait, you want me to do what now – time jump? Oh, I don't know about that. You don't seem to have a great deal of control over this yet. What if we can't get back?"

"We'll only jump back a day or so," Sam said matter-of-factly, like he was talking about going to the nearby neighborhood grocery store for a bottle of milk.

"Mmm. Well, I don't like it, but if it will help you, let's do it."

"OK, Aka, come on down," Sam said in a game show-host voice. "Let's go back a day or two."

"Wait, do I have a choice in this matter?" Akamaru asked. "I mean, geez, I don't even have a dog in this fight...literally! You pulled me out of my basement and sent me centuries back in time. What makes you think I want to do that again?"

Sam looked hurt and embarrassed at the same time. "I apologize," he said meekly. "This is all new to me and I'm not used to talking with and understanding animals. Of course you have a choice. I should have asked if you wanted to do it and I would understand if you don't."

"Ah, it's OK," Akamaru said in a mellow tone. "I'll do it; I just want to have the right to choose."

"You go dog!" Raven said. "Power to the animals! Hey Sam, you don't have to ask me. You know I'll go with you anywhere, anytime, right?"

"Sheesh, stop your brown-nosing," Akamaru chided, the deep rumble returning to his voice.

"Alright, calm down you two. We don't have time for this," Sam interjected. "Thank you Akamaru; it's important that you stay here with Charger and that he can understand you and this is the only way I know to make that happen."

"Let's git 'er done," said Charger as he wheeled over to Sam. Akamaru strode over and sat next to the wheelchair. Charger reached over and placed his hand on the back of the dog's neck. Sam also placed his hand on the dog's neck. Raven jumped to Sam's side and pressed against his leg; he wasn't taking any chances on losing his buddy. Sam had set the dial back what he hoped was two days. He pressed the green button, calling up the light and smoke show.

"Whoa, this is really happening," Charger gasped as he was swirled back two days, and then propelled forward back to the present in the blink of an eye."

"Oh baby, oh baby, that was freakin' amazing!" he said, grinning like a little kid getting off a Disney ride as the lightning broke apart and fell like sparkly sprinkles all around him. "I want to do that again!"

"Newbee," said Akamaru. "You can let go of my fur now."

"Oh dear lord, I do understand you!" Charger exclaimed, looking almost eye to eye with the big dog as he released his death grip on the back of Akamaru's neck.

"Yes, and you should understand me too, so if you need to talk with an intelligent animal I'd be happy to schedule you in, just in case you tire of talking with lower intellectual members of the species," said Raven, winking at Charger and nodding in Akamaru's direction.

"I do understand you Raven, and I appreciate your offer, but I'll be fine here with Akamaru," Charger responded, already feeling a bond forming with the dog.

Sam was amused at Charger's response, but felt a sense of urgency to put the plan into action. "OK Charger, if we aren't back in three days, you know what to do. Let's get this show on the road," said Sam, eager to time jump again; it was kind of addictive.

With that, he put his left arm around Cici's waist, made sure Raven and Lily-Rose were pressed hard against his legs and pulled the remote from his right pocket. Ensuring it was set to AD 80 and hoping they were standing where his parents had been, he looked at Charger and said, "Blastoff."

He pressed the button and Charger was amazed and intrigued as he watched them fade, then disappear in swirling wisps of smoke, sparkling sprinkles and flashes of light all rotating in a funnel. As they faded away he turned to Akamaru and said, "Well, I guess it's just you and me big guy. I say we order a pizza and get started."

"I'm good with that," the dog responded. "I'll take the meat lover's, no peppers or onions and definitely no anchovies."

"Gawd, I can't believe I can understand you. This is so great!" Charger emoted.

"OK, get over it - we better focus on figuring out how to help them if they need it," Akamaru said in his deep, sonorous tone.

"Right, you are absolutely right," Charger said. He called in the pizza order, and then went to the vault where Sam had stashed his parents' notebooks. He opened up time travel notebook number one and began carefully reading. He had three days to learn what the Steelonni's had discovered and devise some way to track where they all were in time; then, find a way to pull them back if needed.

No pressure, Charger thought as he contemplated the enormity of the task. "Guess I won't be getting much sleep in the next seventy-two hours," he said to Akamaru.

"If you don't sleep, I don't sleep," the canine replied. "If fact, even if you sleep, I don't sleep because my job is to keep you safe. I'm on it buddy."

Charger was impressed at the dog's conviction to duty. "That's good to know. This plan...well, it isn't much of a plan and there are about a million ways it wouldn't work, but it's all we have, so...," he trailed off as he began reading the first notebook.

14

TIME TRAVELERS PASSING IN SPACE-TIME

As SAM, RAVEN, CICI AND LILY-ROSE faded from view in the present time hopefully heading back to Rome, AD 80, Tony and Amanda were in an AD 80 Roman alleyway slowly disappearing in a swirl of smoke and sparkling lights as they headed forward in time.

Tony was worried after seeing Sam disappear in the arena. He realized that his son was fiddling with something he didn't understand; something that Tony and Amanda didn't fully understand yet either. So, Tony's normally methodical approach to problems was muddled. He reasoned that since the red home button on their remote didn't work, meaning they couldn't go directly back home from AD 80 to the present, then he'd have to try and jump back – or rather, forward – in increments to their starting point.

He randomly chose 200-year incremental jumps forward as he attempted to hop to the present. Normally, he would have discussed this in detail with Amanda, but there was nothing normal about the situation and he was in a bit of a hurry. So he set AD 280 on the remote, grabbed Amanda's hand and hit the green send button.

"Honey what on earth are you…" Amanda started to say. However, before she could complete her thought, they were immediately engulfed in swirling smoke, sparkling lights, flashes of what appeared to be lightning and a rotating funnel cloud that stretched up at a thirty-degree angle for as far as the eye could see.

Tony and Amanda had the eerie feeling of motion without moving their feet. It was a little nauseating and Tony thought he was going to lose his breakfast. Amanda, on the other hand, became almost child-like in her amazement at the sight. "Oooh, look at all the colors," she said as she reached out to try and touch the sides of the spinning tunnel. Oddly, even though it appeared to be very close, she couldn't touch it.

Tony gently grabbed her hand and pulled it to her side, saying, "Sweetheart, I think it's best if we keep our hands and feet inside the ride and don't touch things until we understand what we're working with here," even though he wanted to do the same thing.

He sensed that his judgement was a bit impaired and he could see that his wife's was as well. It had to relate to their proximity to the green substance, even as small a piece as was in the remote. Another wave of panic jolted him back to reality as he realized that Sam would be experiencing the same lapse in discretion – there was no telling what he might do.

After a few seconds the smoke began to dissipate, the flashes of light faded and they began to see their surroundings. Tony didn't know exactly where they would end up.

He had been a bit surprised that they landed in ancient Rome their first time jump. Since nobody had attempted it before – or at least not that they knew of – there was insufficient data upon which to base a definitive theory.

Tony had first thought that if the remote device had worked it would carry them to the year dialed in, but keep them right in Boston, in the exact spot from which they'd started. When they ended up in the ancient Roman alleyway, he suspected that it was because there was a connection between their minds and the mysterious green substance. Somehow, it knew where they wanted to go just by them thinking it.

However, when he set the dial at AD 280 and hit the green button for a second time, neither of them had a particular destination in mind.

"So, what have you gotten us into this time," Amanda asked as her adult mind took control and she realized she should be concerned. She slapped Tony on his arm and scolded, "Don't ever do that again without telling me first!"

"Sorry about that, I sort of panicked or lost my sense of caution," he conceded. "I think it has something to do with the Amton. I assume we're still in Rome, but now we're in AD 280," he said as he spun the dial to AD 480 and prepared to press the green button again. "Hold on to me, I'm going to jump us up another 200 years," he said, this time giving her fair warning.

He hit the button, but nothing happened. He pressed it again. Nothing.

"Hmmm, looks like we're here for a while, wherever here is," he said apologetically to Amanda. "The good news is we jumped 200 years towards our time. Bad news is, I guess we can't do back-to-back jumps without some down time."

"How much down time?" Amanda asked as she furrowed her brow, widened her eyes and glanced nervously around.

"Great question – I have no idea, I'm kinda' making this up as I go along," Tony replied flatly, wishing he could be a bit more optimistic.

The smoke and sparkles were still settling so they couldn't see clearly for a few more seconds. When they could see, they wished they hadn't.

They were still in the alleyway but now instead of a neat, quiet refuge with reed baskets it was littered in trash and debris and looked as though a cyclone had blown through it. The busy but orderly street that had been in front of them was now embroiled in chaos.

"Looks like we've jumped from the frying pan into the fire," Amanda said. "We're in the middle of a mess. Between AD 235 and 284 the Roman Empire was engulfed in civil war. There were twenty-two emperors during that time and all but two met their demise violently. We need to hide until we can jump out of this time zone. Do you have any idea how long before we'll be able to jump again?"

"Your guess is as good as mine," Tony said, shrugging his shoulders. "Stay close though because I'll keep trying and we have to be touching for us both to jump." He hooked his free hand under her elbow and guided her into an arched doorway along the alleyway.

"Let's see if we can just lay low here until we can jump," Tony said. As they waited he explained his plan, such as it was, to jump 200 years at a time.

"Why 200, and not 400 or 800 years?" she asked, challenging his theory in her usual analytical way.

"I have no idea why," he admitted. "It sounded like a good number at the time, but next time I'll double it and then double it again if that works," he said, dialing AD 680 as people in the street suddenly began screaming in fear.

Amanda peeked around the corner and saw a Roman soldier careening down the street in a horse-drawn chariot. He was lashing a long whip from side to side, taking people down each time it struck.

"We need to get off the street," she told Tony, this time grabbing his arm with one hand as she pulled the handle of the door next to them, hoping it would open and hoping she wasn't leading them into more danger than the whip-yielding soldier presented.

15

TAG TEAMING IN TIME

SAM, CICI, RAVEN AND LILY-ROSE COULD not have known that as they traveled down their time tunnel backwards in time towards Rome 80 A.D., Tony and Amanda were swirling forward in their own tunnel settling in the same place but in 280 A.D.

As the tunnel smoke faded Sam could see they were in an alleyway amidst stacks of woven baskets. They were near the mouth of the alley that emerged into a bustling, but orderly, wide street.

"Holey moley," squealed Cici, clenching her fists and running in place excitedly for a couple of seconds. "That was awesome! I have never felt that totally out of control. I mean it was like riding in the eye of a tornado but not getting pummeled in the process. I do feel a little queasy though."

"Don't worry kid, you'll get used to it when you've time jumped as much as we have," said Raven in his Chicago tough-guy voice.

"Oh geez, you were right, I can understand the cat," she gasped to Sam, as Raven rolled his eyes.

Sam started to say something but Raven jumped in front of him and said, in his best James Cagne accent, "Don't pay attention to what the kid says sister, see, b'cause cats rule!" as he gave her a wink and flipped his long tail in Sam's face.

"Cats can wink?" she said, amazed. "Is that a new thing or have I just missed it all these years?"

"No me'love, I'm faa'rly c'arten I've been 'eable to wink since I was a wee kit'n," said Raven, this time in a light Irish lilt. "Aye, we can do voice impressions too," he added, giving her a big Cheshire smile.

Sam watched the exchange, and then realized he was losing his concentration. "OK Raven, back off before you blow her mind," Sam said, forcefully. The cat and girl snapped their heads in his direction, their eyes wide like they were a child and kitten caught with their hand or paw in the cookie jar. "We've got to focus on the task here."

"Absolutely, yes, you're right, without a doubt," Cici giggled in a gruff voice attempting to imitate Sam's forceful directive, while Raven threw his paw up to his forehead in a crisp salute.

Raven was sitting on top of one of the reed baskets trying to balance as he peeked out at the street. He was still a little woosie after the time jump. The basket wobbled, he lost his balance, slipped backwards, and slammed into Lily-Rose. It was like hitting a brick wall.

"Yeeaouwee!" he squealed, then laughed as he looked up at the cyber-pig. "Thanks for giving me a break – get it, you broke my fall so you gave me a break," he said, laughing at his own joke, though none of the others thought it was funny.

"Sam is right!" spat Lily-Rose in a gruff tone that rumbled and reverberated off the walls of the alley and got everybody's attention, even some people in the street, though all they heard was a pig squealing.

"Thank you Lily," said Sam, shortening the pig's formal name.

"My name is Lily-Rose," she corrected.

Realizing that her protégé was acting like a spoiled brat, Cici took a deep breath to clear her head, then said, "It's OK, he can call you Lily – it's just something he does, shortening names."

"Very well, if you say so, but I do prefer Lily-Rose."

Forgetting for a moment that he was talking to a robo-animal, he said, "I apologize, I will use your full name henceforth."

"Thank you very much Sam," said Lily-Rose, batting her eyelashes and giving Sam a toothy smile.

"So it looks like we got back to ancient Rome, but now where do we start looking for your parents?" Cici asked Sam.

"That is a very good question," he responded, not really having a plan past getting to this point. "I guess we need to think like them and go on instinct. For one thing, we really don't know that they were even here. I was just assuming that because this remote was set for this time. But really, they could have gone anywhere."

As Sam was talking, Raven exercised his cat curiosity and investigated their alleyway. He inspected each reed basket and the two doorways, one on each side in the hand-made brick walls that formed the perimeter of the alleyway. A bright glint from under one basket caught his attention. He pawed at the object that gleamed, then picked it up in his mouth and deposited it at Sam's feet.

"Hey boss, does this look familiar to you?" he said, peering up at Sam and pointing to the object with his left paw. "Because I don't think they made these in ancient Rome."

Sam leaned down and picked it up, then grinned and said, "Nice work Raven! This proves my mother was here. I gave her this bracelet for her birthday. She must have dropped it here…she always did have problems with the clasp. Alright, we know they were here, now we have to figure out where they went."

As Sam spoke he noticed that one of the doors to the alleyway was opened a crack and in the shadows behind the door he thought he saw an eye peering out. He casually drifted over to that side of the alley to try and get a closer look. As he did, the door opened a little farther and the head of a dark-haired, brown-eyed little girl poked out. She was saying something to him, but it was in Latin and she was speaking so fast he didn't understand her. He spoke a little Latin and understood bits and pieces like "two adults" and "smoke and lights."

"Let me talk with her," said Cici, while she grabbed Sam's shirt sleeve and pulled him back so she could kneel down to the little girl's level. She smiled and said, in passable Latin, "Hello there, what's your name?"

Sam's mouth dropped open and he said, "I didn't know you spoke Latin!"

"One of the many mysteries you don't know about me," she said in a rather suggestive tone of voice. "I've studied the language for years…of course, I didn't expect to actually *need* it…but let me see what she knows."

Cici turned back to the girl and they had an animated interchange for several minutes, then Cici said to the girl, *gratias tibi ago*, which literally translated, means, "thanks to you I give."

She stood up and motioned for her three companions to gather round so she wouldn't have to repeat it. "This young lady, Maria, is eight years old and she said that she saw two adults in the alleyway just a few minutes ago and she heard them talking in a strange language she didn't understand – the same as she heard from us. She said they left and walked towards the Colosseum, but they came back in a few minutes and pushed a button and were caught in a storm of swirling smoke and lights, and then they were gone. She said it was very scary."

"Yes, I can identify with that feeling," Sam said, looking at the little girl with a smile. "*Gratias*," he said to Maria, knowing enough Latin to say the short version of thank you. The girl smiled, cast her eyes downward and blushed, clearly impressed by the tall, dark-haired stranger with the deep brown eyes.

"Well, now we know they were here but they left – so where did they go?" asked Raven. Maria heard only a cat meowing and she reached out and stroked Raven's smooth fur. Raven purred instinctively and flicked his tail around to gently brush the little girl's cheek. She giggled.

"I think you found a new friend," Lily-Rose said to Raven. Of course, Maria only heard a pig squeal, making her back up a step. Raven padded over to the pig and rubbed her shoulder with his head, saying, "Lily-Rose, you are scaring the little girl. Go make nice to her."

Lily-Rose gave the cat a blank look, then softened her gaze, put her head down and walked towards the little girl, who backed up a step and hit the wall. "She won't hurt you," Cici said to her in Latin.

The pig reached the little girl and she was nearly eyeball to eyeball with her. Lily-Rose sat down and lowered her head for a pat. The little girl extended her hand, lightly patted the pig's furry head twice then quickly withdrew her hand and tucked it into her pocket.

"Nicely done Lily-Rose," said Sam. "Now, back to my parents. I guess they'd eventually try to get home, but my mom is a card-carrying ancient Rome junkie, so my guess is they went to the Colosseum because she couldn't resist the opportunity. But what made them come back here so quickly and leave again?"

"Maybe they saw something at the Colosseum or along the way that scared them," Cici speculated. "Hey, when did you say you took your little trip to the arena and danced with lions?"

"Umm, that would have been early yesterday morning, why?" said Sam.

"I'm thinking out loud now so bear with me, but from what little I know of time travel theory, time theoretically moves more slowly in a wormhole than in real time," said Cici, crinkling her eyebrows pensively as she tried to sort out her thoughts – a little quirk that Sam thought was really cute. "So while it may seem like just a few minutes in the wormhole, it could be a few hours or even days in real time."

"Yes, I think that is correct," Sam agreed, still not knowing where she was headed with this line of thinking.

"OK, so we know your parents disappeared within twenty-four hours of when you discovered them missing because you saw them the day before, right?" Cici continued, not waiting for an answer. "So, could it be possible that your parents were here at the same time you were facing off with those lions in the arena and could it be possible that they saw you disappear?"

"Hmmm, that's a stretch, but it is possible, I guess," said Sam, shaking his head, looking down and rubbing his chin with his cupped hand, thinking. "However, it's the best explanation I've heard so far. If it's true, then I'd guess they'd try to go home because they'd assume that's where I'd go."

"So maybe we should go back home to see if that's where they went when Maria saw them go up in a puff of smoke," Raven interjected. It still amazed Cici that the animals were so smart!

"Right, what the cat said," Sam nodded in agreement.

Raven sat back, curled his tail around himself and with a self-satisfied grin said in his best Hollywood-actor Oscar-acceptance voice, "Thank you, thank you all, it was really nothing, just me being magnificent... again." This made Cici giggle like a little girl, Sam roll his eyes and Maria grin just because of how funny the cat looked and sounded – Lily-Rose stared blankly, still not comprehending the concept of humor.

"OK, enough frivolity, let's get...," Sam started saying, but was interrupted by a commotion in the street. He peeked out and saw a platoon of Roman soldiers in formation marching down the middle of the street going towards the Colosseum. They were pulling several heavily-muscled men by chains.

What happened next occurred in such rapid succession that later as Sam would look back on it, he would never forgive himself.

The soldiers were about to pass their alley and the time travelers would be in plain sight. "It's time for us to go," he said. "Raven, Lily-Rose, get your paws and hooves on me now!" Raven wasted no time in jamming himself against Sam's leg. Cici had her left hand on Lily-Rose's collar, intending to guide her out of sight. She pulled her towards the wall near the alleyway door.

Thinking Cici was right behind him, Sam intended to step back so he was touching her and hit the home button. It would have worked. However, as he stepped back and his finger was pressing the red button, Maria ran out, grabbed Cici's right hand and yanked her towards the door dragging Lily-Rose with her, away from Sam, whispering, "abeamus, abeamus" meaning, "let's go, let's go," thinking the handsome young man and the large cat would follow.

Tragically, that's not what happened. As Sam and Raven were disappearing in a swirl of smoke and lights, Cici and Lily-Rose were being pulled away from them by the well-intentioned little girl who was trying to save them from the soldiers. Sam realized at the last moment that Cici was no longer touching him. He looked back in horror as she and Lily-Rose faded from his sight in a grey whirlwind.

"Sam, wait," she was shouting, in English, reaching out her hand to him. As Sam swirled, he saw the soldiers marching by their alleyway. Cici's shout drew the attention of the closest soldier, who snapped his helmeted head towards the alley. He saw a small dust storm and would later think he remembered seeing a young man shouting in a strange language and a large cat, but then they faded and all he saw was an empty alley. He marched on; he was not going to tell anybody that he thought he saw a ghost.

"Cici!…" Sam was shouting as he swirled again to see Cici, Lily-Rose and Maria disappear into the alley doorway. Then the alley faded and was lost in the cyclone that took Sam and Raven back home and left Cici and Lily-Rose stranded in Rome, AD 80.

Sam and Raven disappear into a time vortex while Cici and Lily-Rose are accidently left stranded in ancient Rome as they are dragged into a doorway by a little Roman girl.

16

MOLNIKOV'S SCHEME

As SAM, CICI, RAVEN AND LILY-ROSE were in the midst of their situation in the ancient Roman alley way, Ivan Molnikov was preparing to pick the lock on the front door of the Steelonni home.

He had been planning this break-in for weeks as he staked out the house from a common-looking gray Ford Taurus. He would park the car in different places each day along the road near their home, which fortunately was a several-acre estate on a side road with minimal traffic, so nobody noticed him.

He watched the coming and going at the home, observing that Tony and Amanda went into the house one day and didn't come out again. Then he saw their son, Sam, in the house with a dog and cat, followed by a young girl entering the house in a big hurry. She went in with her pet pig and never came back out. Then a boy in a wheelchair went back and forth to his home next door, taking the dog with him.

Molnikov knew something was going on in that house and he needed to see what it was.

So on the fourth day he finally decided to take a chance and break in the house. After he saw the wheelchair boy and the dog leave at three o'clock in the afternoon, he walked up to the front door with a tool box in his hand. Anyone who might see him would think he was just a workman getting ready to do some sort of project at the home.

When he got to the door he looked behind him and on both sides and didn't see anybody. So he removed the lock picking device he had in his pants pocket and kneeled down to pick the lock; it took him about ten seconds and the door creaked open a crack.

Patting himself mentally on the back, he slid the lock pick back into his pocket, stood up, looked around again and seeing nobody he picked up his tool box, pushed open the door, stepped quietly inside, gently pushed the door closed and turned the lock from the inside.

The house was dark and very quiet. He heard a clock ticking somewhere deep in the bowels of the colonial style home. His footsteps echoed even though he was treading lightly. The entry foyer opened into a large family room that had a big, comfy sofa in front of a seventy-two-inch flat screen TV hanging on the wall. The rest of the room was tastefully decorated and furnished.

"How I hate these opulent Americans," he whispered to himself in his strong Russian accent, thinking how this home contrasted starkly with his dank, one-bedroom apartment and twenty-three-inch, 1990s-era TV that barely worked. It's not that he wouldn't have had a large, five-bedroom home like theirs if he could, but he didn't because the Steelonni's kept beating him to inventions and depriving him of the monetary rewards that followed. He was nearly broke.

He had to blame someone and he knew it could not possibly be his fault, so he blamed Tony and Amanda Steelonni. In his twisted mind, he justified breaking into their home and stealing whatever secrets they had hidden; and if someone had to be hurt in the process, well, he could justify that as well.

"I will find whatever this green, glowing substance is. I will take it because they owe it to me for all the times they have beaten me to inventions and stolen my rewards," he thought to himself, as he set the tool box down near the front door and quietly padded from room to room.

The house was very quiet. He saw the source of the ticking; a large grandfather clock stood watch over the formal living room. Tick, Tock...Tick Tock; it nearly drove him crazy listening to it. He stopped to admire the tasteful decorations in the living room; then spat a curse at himself in Russian for giving credit to his rivals and the finery that should be his.

He sensed a strange smell in the air. It was the pungent odor of a strong electrical charge, similar to the smell of a close lightning strike. It reminded him of the odor produced by his experiments to develop a weapon that would fire a powerful electric bolt across a room; he was in fact carrying the prototype with him, just in case. He reached down to his side and patted the grip of the holstered, pistol-like weapon the size of a large handgun. He smiled to himself, knowing he would not hesitate to fry anyone who got in his way.

The house was too quiet. He knew there should be at least four people, a cat, a dog and a pig in the house making some sort of noise. But there was nothing.

After checking the main level and the upstairs, he found the basement door and tried to creep quietly down the steps, but his excessive weight made each stair tread screech in protest. It didn't help that sweat poured off his oily forehead into his eyes, blurring his vision and making him stumble more than walk down the stairs.

He thought surely the racket he was making would alert somebody in the house, but when he got down to the basement floor he could see the entire space and there was nobody in it. He wandered aimlessly around the basement laboratory careful not to pick anything up or disturb the tools and equipment. He didn't want anyone to know he'd been here.

He saw no evidence of a glowing green substance or anything that hinted at what they were working on. He was pondering his next move, scanning the basement to find something to give him a lead, when his eyes saw, way back in the corner, the large, steel door of a walk-in safe built into the wall.

"Ah ha!" he whispered to himself as he guided his girth through the narrow isles between work tables towards the safe. "So this is where they keep their secrets."

When he got to the closed safe door he reached out his hand, put it on the opening lever and pushed down…nothing. It was shut tighter than a clamshell. In frustration, he grabbed the handle with both hands, pulling it and shaking it hard, causing sweat the sling off his forehead onto the floor…still, it did not budge.

"*Govno*," he cursed in a raspy Russian accent. He was about to let loose with a string of other Russian cursing he'd learned on the whaling ships. He stopped when he felt pressure on his ears. The smell that had been faint in the air upstairs now began to get stronger.

He turned around in time to see a whirlwind forming in the middle of the basement floor. There were flashes of red, green, blue, orange and other colored lights. It was like a miniature thunderstorm forming in the basement, but the electrical flashes didn't scorch anything; it was more like heat lighting, lots of light but no impact.

Molnikov thought he saw bodies in the middle of the storm. Then, as the flashes of light began to fade and the whirling smoke and dust cleared, he could see a young man and a large cat solidifying in front of him.

Molnikov instinctively drew the electric shock gun from its holster and pointed it at the boy.

Sam was horrified. He had left his best friend and her pet robo-pig in an ancient Roman alley!

"Raven we've got to go back," he said desperately, fumbling to reset the remote. He had his back to Molnikov, but Raven was facing him and said to Sam, "Uh, amigo, I think that guy there with the funny-looking gun might not be in favor of you leaving just yet."

Sam was shocked to hear a man behind him say in a strong Russian accent, "You are not going anywhere unless I say you can, young man!"

Sam whirled around, slipping his hand holding the remote into his trouser pocket as he did so. He saw a man holding an odd-looking pistol pointed at his chest. Instead of a barrel, the gun had two electrodes sticking out the front. He wasn't sure what kind of gun it was, but he figured it wasn't going to shoot out rose pedals or one of those "bang" banners if the man pulled the trigger.

So, as always trying to stay cool but stuttering a little just the same, Sam said to the man, "Hi thu-thu-there, I think you may have taken a wro-wrong turn at the Russian embassy. Care to tell me what you are doing in muh-my house?"

Molnikov barely noticed the stuttering. He admired Sam's flippant attitude under pressure. "I will not hesitate to send 50,000 volts through your body if you do not do exactly as I say," Molnikov said to Sam, exaggerating his Russian accent because he knew that intimidated some Americans. Sam only chuckled because it reminded him of Boris on the old *Rocky and Bullwinkle* cartoons.

"Ah, I can tell from your accent you're not from around here – maybe once we get to know each other I could take you for a tour," Sam said without missing a beat. "Have you ever seen Fenway Park – it's awesome. Buh-By the way, who are you and wh-why are you in my house pointing a – what, a ray gun at me?"

Sam's lack of fear both impressed and infuriated Molnikov. "I will ask the questions. Where are your parents?"

"Well, you know, that is an interesting question. As a matter of fact, I've been asking that same question. I don't know where they are either."

"You are lying," spat Molnikov, his voice full of menace; but, at the same time Sam discerned a little bit of a whine in there too. He could tell this man, who he believed was Dr. Molnikov, didn't have a clue what was really going on and that he was frustrated. Sam decided to play that hand and see where it got him. He was stalling for time as he devised an escape plan.

"No, I am not lying, I've been looking all over for them and nary a hair on their head have I found. Do you have any idea where they might be?"

"You lying little cur, I just saw you materialize out of thin air and you are trying to tell me you don't know what is going on?"

"Ha-hah-hah, what, oh that?" Sam said, over-emphasizing a "ha-hah" laugh, pointing back to where he had materialized. "That is just a smoke and mirrors trick I was working on. I am a weekend magician, do little tricks for the neighbor kids. I do birthday parties and bar mitzvahs, in fact I have a card here somewhere…"

Sam fumbled in his pockets and turned around to face the workbench like he was looking for his card. As he turned he pulled the remote from his pocket so the man couldn't see him do it. He glanced down to make sure it was still set for 80 A.D. and as he did he made sure his leg was touching Raven. Then, hoping he'd disappear before he was zapped, and hoping he'd go right back to that Roman alley, he punched the green button.

Molnikov realized what was happening as he saw the boy and the cat fading and being engulfed by plumes of smoke. As the multi-colored lights began to sparkle around him, Molnikov raised the pistol and pulled the trigger. Nothing happened. The Russian looked down and realized that the safety was still on. He flipped it off and as he looked back up and pulled the trigger, Sam was looking over his shoulder, smiling and waving "bye bye" with his fingers as the cat's tail flipped around his neck and the two of them disappeared from sight.

The lightning bolt from the gun flew across the room and did serious damage to the wall. But the boy and cat were already gone, leaving Molnikov pointing his weapon at empty air and cursing the entire Steelonni family.

17

CICI, LILY-ROSE AND MARIA

Cici normally kept a pretty cool head and was not prone to freaking out, but when Maria grabbed her hand and pulled her and Lily-Rose from the alleyway at the same time she saw Sam and Raven going up in a puff of smoke – she FREAKED out.

"Oh great!" she spurt out, while several other more colorful comments rolled around in her head waiting to exit her mouth. But they stopped when Maria squeezed her hand tightly and harshly whisper, "*Conquiesco!*"

She could understand Latin so she knew Maria was telling her, in a nice way, to shut up. Cici clamped her hand over her mouth to let Maria know she understood. As they crouched in a corner among wine boxes behind the closed and locked door, Cici saw a shadow darken the window. She wrapped her arm around Lily-Rose's neck and said, "Be very quiet." A Roman soldier who had heard or seen something in the alley had decided to investigate.

The two girls and the pig held their breath as the soldier rattled the door knob. Thankfully, Maria had the presence of mind to slide the lock as she was pulling them into the room. The soldier cupped his hands over his eyes and tried to peer into the room, but the lights were out and it was in almost total shadows. Someone yelled to the soldier from the street, so he had to give up his search and scurry to catch up with his troops.

Once the pounding, rhythmic sound of the marching soldiers faded into the distance, Maria turned to Cici and said, in Latin, "We should be safe now. The soldiers only come through here two or three times a day so it will be quite a while before they come again."

"*Gratias tibi ago*" Cici said. Continuing in Latin, she added, "I am so grateful to you for saving me. Is this your home?"

"Yes it is. I live here with my mother and father and my two brothers," said Maria, giving Cici a big, sweet smile. "My Papa is a very important man and my Mama is very beautiful."

Cici was totally taken by the adorable little Roman girl, but she was still FREAKING OUT about being left behind. She knew Sam still didn't have his time-jumping down with any degree of certainty, so there was no guarantee he'd be able to come back for her. She decided the best thing she could do was find out more about Maria and her family.

"What does your father do?" she asked Maria.

"He is an important man at the Colosseum. He is the one who makes sure everything is in order so that the gladiators and the animals are all ready for the fighting. He has been away for three days in Milonia to find more *bestiarri*," Maria told Cici. "They are special, very brave gladiators who fight animals."

How pleasant, thought Cici, so her father is the guy who arranges the daily carnage show that almost consumed Sam. She must have shown concern that Maria saw because the little girl quickly said, "Oh, don't worry, my Papa said I am too young to watch the games but that nobody really gets hurt or is eaten, it is all make believe." The white lies that daddies tell their little girls to protect them, thought Cici. She really doubted that the accounts of history were so wrong that the "games" in the Colosseum could be compared to the *World Wrestling Entertainment* show. She was pretty sure that body slams and bone-crunching were not faked in the Roman arena.

Wanting to change the subject, Cici asked Maria about her home. "Is your home bigger than just this room?"

"Oh, yes, yes, it is beautiful. This is just a back way to the alley. Let me show you the house!"

Cici didn't really want to go far from the room in case Sam was able to jump back for her. But she was hungry and was hoping Maria would show her to the kitchen. Cici motioned for Lily-Rose to follow as they walked up a short flight of stairs. It got brighter and brighter as they neared the top.

The stairs widened out to a home that truly was beautiful. It was apparent that her parents were doing pretty well for themselves. Cici recalled from her reading of history that in ancient Rome, only the wealthy could afford single-family homes, which were called domus.

There were beautiful white columns, high ceilings, marble floors and gorgeous wood accents with plants and flowers everywhere. It was exactly like pictures Cici had seen in history books. The archeologists and historians had nailed it describing the inside of Roman homes. Wouldn't they just love to see this for themselves, she thought.

Thankfully, the kitchen was just off a large central area and it was then that Cici realized there wouldn't be a fridge to open up and grab some lunch meat and a cold drink. Instead, Maria pulled a loaf of freshly-baked bread and a block of sharp-cheddar cheese from a pantry and cut slices of each for Cici. It was delicious.

Maria went deeper into the pantry and returned with a decanter that had a red drink in it. She poured a glass into a wine chalice and handed it to Cici, who put it up to her lips but sniffed it first. "This is wine!" she said to Maria.

"Yes, it is. The grapes were grown in our family vineyard and my Mama made the wine. It is very good."

Cici remembered that wine was a staple drink in ancient Rome. Even children drank it with their meals.

"Hmmm," thought Cici as she put the chalice to her lips and took a sip. It was surprisingly cool, sweet and delicious. "I think I could get used to living here," she thought. Cici was famished and she ate the sliced bread and cheese as Maria filled the chalice two more times.

By the time she was done eating…and drinking…Cici was very, very happy. She had never had that much wine. She had only sipped some of her mother's once at a family wedding.

By the end of the first glass, she was feeling pretty relaxed. She and Maria had a very nice conversation about Maria's life; Cici had to be careful not to talk too much about her own life because it would only confuse Maria.

"Is your pig a war pig?" Maria asked as she stroked Lily-Rose's soft, synthetic fur; if Maria suspected the fur wasn't real, she gave no sign of it. Cici remembered reading about war pigs. Pigs were a rather unconventional weapon used in ancient Roman warfare.

War pigs were supposedly used as a countermeasure against war elephants, Cici remembered from her studies. Carthaginian war elephants engaged Roman infantry at the Battle of Zama as early as 202 BC and provided a significant tactical advantage on the battlefield. However, elephants were afraid of squealing pigs, so the Romans began using them with great effect. When Carthaginian's began training their elephants with young pigs, Romans sent flaming war pigs in to scare elephants. It was brutal but effective.

"Oh, no, no, Lily-Rose is my pet, my friend," Cici said, causing the pig to rub her head on Cici's leg to demonstrate. Cici was amazed to see that her little AI pig was learning to be affectionate.

By the end of the second glass of wine, Cici noticed that she was kind of slurring her words a little. Her Latin was getting sloppy and she accidently threw in a few English words, which Maria either didn't notice or ignored.

By the end of the third glass it was too late for her to realize she was sloshed. How could such a sweet, wonderful drink make her feel so, well, so out of control. She was laughing way too much at things Maria said that weren't really all that funny. But she just felt so good.

How, she wondered, did ancient Roman people get anything done if they drank wine with their meals?

Cici also realized that another side-effect of the wine was that she had to go to the bathroom…badly. She politely asked Maria where she could urinate and then she sort of freaked out again when she realized her idea of a bathroom and ancient Rome's were two different things.

Maria showed her to a room with one small, high window and in the corner was an ornate marble chair with a hole in the seat and a ceramic pail under it. Cici remembered reading about this. Romans didn't have toilet paper; they used tree leaves or moss, or in some cases a spongia. This was literally a sponge on a stick. At this point, it could have been sand paper and she'd have been OK with that because she just had to GO.

When Cici was swirled into this time period she found herself clad in a tunic, a garment like a long, ankle-length tee-shirt, with nothing underneath. So to use the bathroom all she had to do was just hike it up in back and sit on the cold marble seat, leaving the front of the tunic to cover her knees and her modesty.

When she had finished her business, she rinsed the spongia in a channel of running water at her feet and pushed it through a hole at the front, wiped her privates, then rinsed off the spongia and left it in a basin for the next person to use. She assumed that Maria's family had "people" who would empty the ceramic pail.

"Well, that could have been worse," she thought as she stumbled out of the room, much refreshed but still pretty woozy. Lily-Rose was waiting for her. "Feel better?" she asked with obvious concern that surprised Cici; she had attempted to program the AI pig to learn emotion but didn't realize she would learn it so quickly.

She knew it was time for them to get back to the little room off the alley because she didn't need any more wine. However, she got turned around when she left the bathroom and ended up in a large, bright atrium.

As she stood in the middle of the room she shielded her eyes, a bit disturbed by the light, swaying slightly. As she looked up at the plants and flowers, a large door opened and a barrel-chested, muscular, dark-haired man ambled through. As he closed the door, he looked up to see Cici and the pig. He stopped dead in his tracks.

"*Quis es tu?*" or, "Who are you," he said in a very controlled but threatening tone, pointing a very thick, hairy arm at them. He reminded Cici of every Mafia hit-man she'd ever seen on TV. He might was well have said in a Chicago accent, "Hey, who da'heck ah'you?"

Cici, whose blood alcohol content far exceeded sensible speaking limits, was speechless. She just gawked at him with wide deer-in-the-headlights eyes, her mouth gaped opened and her brain scrambling feverishly to form a coherent sentence.

Thankfully, Maria came to the rescue, popping out of the kitchen with a giggle and a grin, running to her daddy and jumping into his burly arms saying, "Papa, welcome home, this is my friend Cecilia, but she is called Cici for short and that is her pig, Lily-Rose."

The big hairy man turned into a big, hairy puppy the minute Maria came into the room. He beamed with an ear-to-ear grin and said, "So where did you meet your new friend?" Cici could see that behind the smile Papa was still suspicious of the strangers in his house. "She and her pig were in the alley when the soldiers were coming and since they are strangers in the city they would have taken them so I saved them," Maria said with innocence and sincerity, as she batted her long, dark eyelashes at her father, unconsciously wrapping the brute around her little finger.

"So, Cici, where are you from and what brought you to our alleyway?" Papa asked Cici directly. It was a fair question to ask someone who has invaded your home, even if your eight-year-old daughter invited them in. The real answer would have been unbelievable to Papa, so Cici was formulating a watered-down version of the truth when Maria came to the rescue again.

"She and Lily-Rose have come from far away and they are not familiar with our city so they got lost and separated from their friends," the little dark-haired angel told her father, so honestly because that's what she believed.

That story was exactly the version of reality that Cici was going for, so she jumped in on her own behalf, hoping her Latin was good enough to fool the man. "That's right, I came from Cremona to visit my cousins and while we were out exploring the city we got caught up in a big crowd near the Colosseum and were swept away from our friends."

Papa listened to her and when she was done he just stood looking her directly in the eyes for what seemed like many minutes, but was only a few seconds. Cici remembered what her father had taught her about bluffing in poker – when you're bluffing, make eye contact with your opponent and don't blink. So that's what she did – and finally he blinked, and smiled.

"Well, I am happy Maria found you and brought you into our home!" he said, stretching his arms out to his sides with open hands and sweeping them side to side in a welcoming gesture that indicated he believed her story…at least until he had no reason not to. "My name is Giuseppe Cartonia."

Just then, there was a loud, insistent knock on his door that sent him flying to find out who dared interrupt the solitude of his home.

As he flung open the door, a man excitedly asked forgiveness for the interruption but there was pandemonium at the Colosseum – one of the gladiators had disappeared – just disappeared in a puff of smoke and lightning – right before the crowd's eyes.

"Preposterous!" exclaimed Mr. Cartonia. "People don't just disappear."

Cici watched the interchange, wondering if perhaps this was a delayed reaction to Sam-the-gladiator's disappearing act. Mr. Cartonia had been gone for several days and Sam had told her that minutes or hours in time travel would equal days or weeks in normal time.

So it was possible that though only a few hours had elapsed for them in time travel, a few days had gone by here and since Mr. Cartonia had been away he was just getting the news.

"*Veniam in me*," he said, excusing himself to Cici and his daughter, "I must go find out what is going on. Maria, tell Mama that I will be home as soon as I can." With that, he whisked out the door, slamming it a bit too hard as he left.

His exit gave Cici the opening she was looking for. "Maria, you've been very kind to help me, but I must get back to the alleyway to be there when my friend comes for me," she said.

"Yes, how will he come for you? I didn't see him and the big cat leave but they must have a horse and wagon, correct?" Maria asked with innocence only a young child would have.

"Yes, something like that," Cici responded, knowing Maria could not witness a time-travel rescue because she just would not understand. For that matter, Cici still didn't understand it; she just knew it was possible.

"Maria, you must stay here in case my friend comes to the front door," Cici said, giving Maria a little hug, then rushing back to the little room off the alleyway, Lily-Rose on her heels. She didn't relish the thought of waiting in the alley, but she knew if Sam did make it back they would only have a few seconds to grab each other and get out.

She looked back and saw Maria wave and smile, but she stayed where she was. That was good. Cici didn't want to expose the innocent girl to any more danger. She got to the little room and slowed down because it was dark in there. She quietly cracked the door open and was relieved to see that the alley was empty and the street it intersected was quiet. She did hear quite a commotion coming from the Colosseum.

Knowing Sam would try to get back quickly, she stepped into the alley, closed the door and backed against the wall, waiting.

18

HOMEWARD BOUND

In AD 280, Amanda gripped her husband's sleeve in her right hand as she pushed with her left on the door from the alleyway. To her surprise and relief, it opened. She stepped in, pulled Tony with her, and then closed the door quickly just as the soldier in the chariot whipped by the alleyway. He looked that way, but all he saw was an empty alley.

It was very dark in the room. As their eyes adjusted to the meager light that filtered through cracks in wooden shutters that covered the only window, they could see they were in a storage room. Wooden crates were scattered across the dirt floor, some stacked, some toppled over. On the side of one of the boxes, in Latin, Amanda read out loud, "Rome, Italy, Colosseum, wine."

"Hmm, looks like we ended up in the Colosseum's wine storage room," she said to Tony.

"Under different circumstances, I'd say it's five o'clock somewhere and time for a glass of really old wine, but our judgement is already impaired so I think we should pass, for now anyway," he said, picking up a bottle and reading the production date, 278. "I wonder if we took this bottle back to the 21st century, if that would disrupt the space-time continuum," he asked, only half-joking, because he really did want to take it back to sample wine from the 3rd century.

Amanda frowned and said sternly, "Do you really want to test that theory and possibly destroy the world we know?"

Giving that some thought, he gently put the bottle back in the box and said, "Well, when you put it that way, yeah, it does sound like a really bad idea."

He had been pushing the green button every few seconds as Amanda was navigating them out of the alley, but either the device was malfunctioning, or it needed more down time before it was ready to jump them 400 years into the future.

"I think the TimeCon needs a few minutes to re-boot between jumps," he said, shaking it up and down as though that would help it recharge. "It's been nearly five minutes and it hasn't done anything but click when I push the button."

"All we can do at this point is hope it doesn't take much longer because it's only a matter of time before someone finds us," Amanda cautioned.

As if on cue, the words were just out of her mouth when the inner door to the wine cellar opened and a young woman holding a candle walked down the three stairs and began searching through the boxes. The two time travelers huddled quietly behind a stack of boxes, hoping she'd find what she was looking for and leave.

No such luck. Her search brought her closer and closer to them. Tony was unconsciously still pushing the green button and the lady stopped as she heard the "click, click" sound. Amanda grabbed his hand and stopped him…too late. The lady lifted her candle high and the couple was illuminated by its soft glow. The lady gasped and took a step back.

Amanda stood up, her hands palm out in front of her in a non-threatening gesture, and in Latin she hoped would pass the test of time, she said, "Hello, please don't be frightened. We mean you no harm. We are strangers to Rome and we lost our way so we found your door opened and were hiding from the soldiers." Tony stood up next to her, smiling, hiding the TimeCon in his trouser pocket.

The lady looked at them for a long few seconds, deciding whether to scream or to stay calm. But as she searched their faces, she sensed they were not a threat. She decided to trust them.

"I understand, please come with me," she said with a sweet, calm voice that gave Tony and Amanda hope that they would be her guests, not her prisoners. They followed her up the stairs, from near darkness to a bright sunny room filled with paintings, flowers and furniture made from wood and marble.

Amanda knew this was the home of someone with considerable wealth because chairs had arms, couches had cushions and tables displayed fine pottery and sculptures. Through her studies of ancient Roman culture, she knew that the large reclining couches, known as lectus, and sculptures were not a luxury the average citizen could afford.

"Please, sit down," the lady said, as though they were neighbors over for a visit with a friend rather than strangers who showed up in her wine cellar. She went to a long marble side table and poured two glasses of red wine from a beautiful glass decanter. She handed them each a crystal glass and poured one for herself. Amanda knew that sharing wine was a sign of cordiality.

"Hey, I get to drink the wine anyway," Tony whispered in English through his teeth to Amanda out the side of his mouth, keeping the smile plastered on his face. His Latin was rusty to non-existent.

"*Ignosce mihi*," the lady asked, meaning "Pardon me?"

Jabbing Tony sharply in his ribs with her elbow, she said to the lady, "Please excuse my husband's bad manners. He is from a faraway land and does not speak Latin well. He said that you are very kind to allow us into your home and offer us your wine." She smiled at the lady, then dipped her eyebrows and shot a sideways frown at Tony.

"It is my pleasure," the lady said. "I am Valeria Cartonia and this is my father's house. He is in charge of operations at the Colosseum, a job that has been handed down for generations, since my great-great grandfather Giuseppe Cartonia first held this position. We welcome friendly strangers to our home."

"You are very gracious to do so," Amanda said as Tony smiled and nodded his head in agreement with whatever his wife had just said.

"Please let me show you our home," Valeria said as she motioned with a sweeping gesture of her arm. They followed her from room to room. Amanda was as giddy as a little kid, not believing that she was walking through an actual Roman home in AD 280. Archeologists would give anything for this opportunity.

The home was magnificent. It had been expanded through the years, older sections retaining the original architecture and newer parts showing upgrades. Furniture was marble, iron, wood or combinations of those materials. The window draperies were exquisite, made from materials Amanda could not identify.

When they entered an expansive foyer that led to a huge wooden exterior door, Amanda was immediately drawn to a series of paintings on the nearest wall. They were so well done that they almost looked like photographs. She stepped over to get a closer look and as she studied them, she suddenly gave a little gasp.

"What's wrong?" Tony whispered.

"Look at these paintings and tell me what you think," she said, regaining her composure and smiling at him, as Ms. Cartonia watched them with curious interest.

Tony drew closer and examined the paintings; then his eyes widened too. "I see what you mean," he said. "Ask her about the history of these paintings."

"These are amazing paintings; can you tell me about their history?" Amanda asked.

"Ah, those are family heirlooms passed down for four generations," she said. "They were painted by an artist who was a close friend of my great-great grandfather. They represent two very interesting family stories, well, mysteries really. One was told by Guiseppe's daughter, my great-great aunt Maria. She said that, when she was a child, she was visited by two strangers, a young man and woman, who had a unique cat and a pig. This is hard to believe, but she said that the boy and cat disappeared in a whirlwind with lightning and the girl and pig were left behind, but they eventually vanished too.

As she was telling the story, Amanda and Tony were studying the painting. It showed all the things she was describing. While the figures were too small to really show facial features, the tawny-colored cat with the long tail was a close match for Raven. They looked at each other silently passing an "OMG!"

"The other painting is based on a story Guiseppe told about an incident at the Colosseum," Valeria continued. "He did not witness this himself because he was away at the time, but he heard it enough

Sam's mother, Amanda, and father, Tony, look at amazing, and disturbing, paintings in an ancient Roman home.

from so many of the Colosseum's staff and spectators that he was able to recount it to the painter. It shows a *bestiarri* who was fighting two lions when he just disappeared in a whirlwind filled with smoke and lightning. It caused quite a commotion and the Colosseum was closed for many days to investigate, but nobody ever determined what happened. The interesting thing is, as you can see, the same odd-looking cat appeared in both stories."

Tony leaned in to the second painting and it was his turn to gasp as he saw Raven in front of the gladiator and a dog behind him. He immediately recognized the scene as the same one he'd seen when he and Amanda were in the Colosseum.

It left no doubt in Tony's mind. These paintings clearly showed Raven and that meant that both the gladiator and the boy who visited Guiseppe's house was Sam. The girl with him had to be Cici, who was always getting caught up in Sam's escapades; the flaming red hair was a strong indicator. He didn't know where the pig came from, but he knew this meant their son was trying to find them and was getting deep into something he didn't understand; something that could be dangerous.

He knew that Sam wouldn't stop trying until he found them no matter what the cost. They had to get home before something really bad happened.

"Tell her we need to go, *now*," Tony said to Amanda, who started to object until she saw the intense look on his face. She knew that look and she knew he'd be pushing that button any moment. Sam and Cici had already left their time-traveling footprints on history and she didn't want to create another family mystery.

Amanda had figured out the paintings too, so without protest she turned to Valeria, thanked her for a wonderful time, and said that they had imposed on her enough, but had to leave.

Being a good hostess, Valeria quickly wrapped a loaf of fresh bread, a block of cheese, and two bottles of wine into a cloth and handed it to them.

"Can I help you find any certain place in the city?" she asked Amanda?

"Oh, thank you, but we know where we are and where we are going now, so we must be on our way because we have people waiting for us," Amanda replied.

As they were talking Tony was ushering them closer to the door and when Amanda stopped talking, he pushed down the handle, opened the door, and grabbed her elbow to half-push, half-drag her out. Amanda smiled over her shoulder and waved to Valeria as they turned a corner and she disappeared from view.

They were in a courtyard outside the house that was surrounded by a tall wrought iron fence that faced a deserted street.

"Grab on to me and hang on," Tony said. She did it; then he pushed the red home button below the LED readout that read 680 A.D. The TimeCon worked and with a whoosh in a kaleidoscope-whirlwind they made a clean getaway; or so they thought.

From an upstairs window, peeking from behind laced curtains, Valeria stood wide-eyed, her mouth gaped open in amazement, as she watched the two strangers in her courtyard disappear before her eyes in a whirl of smoke and flashing multi-colored lightning.

It was an unbelievable story she would later divulge to her father, who then commissioned a well-known artist to document it in another painting, to add to their extraordinary collection.

19

EIFFEL TOWER, PYRAMIDS AND DINOSAURS

THEORETICALLY, WHEN SAM HIT THE GREEN button to escape from Molnikov's electrode gun, he should have been cycloned back to AD 80 Rome, where he had tragically left Cici and Lily-Rose. However, the theory of time travel was still just that, a theory that hadn't been tested. In a perfect world there would have been years of testing, experimentation and documentation by highly-qualified physicists and other scientists. However, Sam had skipped over that part and gone directly to advanced field testing using a hand-held device his parents had devised.

So, when he set AD 80 on the TimeCon, he expected to see a deserted alleyway; he was shocked, awed and sad simultaneously when the smoke and light of the time tunnel cleared and he found himself craning his head up. Th e sight he beheld was literally the last thing he expected to see; it was the Eiff el Tower in France.

"What the heck have I gone and done now," he said to Raven. Sam looked down at the device and it was set on AD 80 but judging from the scene before him, it clearly was not; and while they had landed on the correct continent, they were in the wrong time period and country. He and Raven had been deposited amidst a store yard of construction equipment and heavy metal girders.

Raven arched his head up too and without taking his eyes off the impressive sight he said, "Uh, boss, I know I'm just a cat and you're supposed to be the highly-intelligent being with opposable thumbs and all that; but, I don't think this is ancient Rome…just sayin…," he trailed off, stopping when he looked at Sam and saw the shocked expression on his face.

Sam's brain still whirled from the spinning time tunnel as he tried to figure out what had happened. He craned his neck up to see the two iron support columns spanned by the iron- latticed arch spanning across Champs de Mar, in Paris.

But there was something wrong. Instead of continuing gracefully up nearly 1,000 feet to what would appear from the ground to be a point, the two sides arched and stopped halfway up, ending in open sky.

Digging back in his memory Sam recalled that the tower had been built as a centerpiece of the 1889 Exposition Universelle, a world's fair designed to celebrate the French Revolution's centennial. It was initially criticized by some intellectuals and leaders as a blight upon the Parisian landscape. But its design was validated when it became a world-wide cultural icon for France and one of the most-visited attractions in the world.

"No, we're definitely not in Rome and definitely not in AD 80," Sam finally responded to Raven, who had been holding his breath waiting, knowing that Sam's big brain was working on the problem. "We are in Paris and I believe it's sometime in 1888. This is the Eiffel Tower about halfway into construction."

"Obvious question here, but how the heck did that happen?" Raven asked, not intending to set Sam off, but doing it anyway.

"I don't know," Sam gasped. "I don't know what I'm doing, OK? I set it for AD 80 and pushed the green button and ka-boom we end up in Paris 1888. So, sue me but I'm doing the best I can here."

Raven knew his buddy was pretty freaked out. "I'm sorry Sam, I wasn't being a smarty cat…it was a stupid question," Raven said, putting his paw on Sam's back and giving a soft pat.

"No, it's the best question to ask, it's just that I don't know the answer," Sam said in a frustrated tone. "Time travel isn't something I've studied, not exactly my area of expertise. However, I have listened to my parents talk about the theories and I think I know what might have happened."

Raven waited a few seconds, but Sam just kept looking up, so he rubbed against Sam's leg to get his attention and said, "OK, curious cat here…so what do you think happened?"

"Well, as best I can recall, time tunnels theoretically open from point to point, but they don't necessarily stay in one place, they can actually move around. They might connect two time points for a minute or a day or a month or a century, but then again they can jump to another point from second to second."

The big cat tried to absorb that concept. He understood, but didn't like it.

"So you're saying we have no definite way to get back to Cici and Miss Piggy?"

Raven was sorry he asked that question when he saw how it affected Sam, who clenched his fists, narrowed his eyes and said in a controlled voice, "No! We don't! But we've got to keep trying." Sam grabbed a handful of fur on Raven's neck and hit the green button; "Here we go again…" Raven yowled.

Smoke, flashing lights, sparkles, the swirling tunnel and then as the dust settled it was clear they had missed their mark again. They stood in hot sand and were smothered by a wave of heat that literally took away their breath. However, the scene in front of them was even more breathtaking.

Rising up from the sand were three structures Sam did know quite a bit about; the Pyramids at Giza – three structures built in the third century BC that still stood mostly intact, except for the damage from climate and vandals. However, the pyramids they saw in front of them were new and nearly unblemished. In fact, the structure nearest them was still under construction.

Sam's voice was filled with anxiety as he told Raven, "These pyramids were built by three different Egyptian pharaohs between 2550 and

2490 BC. Pharaoh Khufu built the tallest one in the middle first; the one behind it by Khafre and the one in front still under construction by Menkaure."

Sam's anxiety slackened as he became more engrossed in the scene before him. "This is one of the Seven Wonders of the Ancient World and we are standing here watching it being built," Sam said, his attention and eyeballs glued high to the hill less than one hundred yards away, where thousands of workers scrambled like worker bees on a hive.

Raven's attention, however, was focused lower and in front of him and he didn't like what he saw.

"Sam, I'm happy that you're happy, but if you'll shift your gaze downward you will see what appears to be some very angry Egyptians heading towards us at a high rate of speed."

Sam reluctantly dropped his focus to the ground and his eyes changed from dreamy amazement to sheer panic in an instant.

"Whoa, where'd they come from?" he blurted. A dozen or more heavily-armed Egyptian warriors were barreling down on them, some on horses, some in chariots. They were armed with spears, crossbows and spiked wheels on the chariots.

"Hate to miss meeting those guys but it's time to go…grab on Raven!"

The big cat didn't need a second invitation. He pressed against Sam's knees and wrapped his tail around his neck as a crossbow bolt slammed into the sand in front of them. Sam pressed the green button and took one last longing glance at the pyramids. Then they were gone as spears sliced through the air where they'd been a moment ago.

The Egyptian warriors were baffled and would later tell the story, which soon became a local legend, about a boy and cat who were there one moment and gone in a whirlwind of smoke and light the next. The warriors thought they had been visited by gods.

Hoping this time they'd actually make it back to AD 80 Rome and be able to retrieve their friends, Sam and Raven waited helplessly in the out-of-control time tunnel. The tunnel took an extra-long time, but finally after about five minutes it started to slow and sparkle and clear up but their hope was sadly disappointed.

They found themselves in a dark forest of enormous trees, bushes and plants of all kinds, larger than any they had ever seen. The sounds were fascinating and frightening; animal sounds, insect sounds, water running, wind blowing – it was overwhelming.

Then another sound made the others pale in comparison. There was a primal roar and the ground shook as the trees and bushes behind them were either pushed aside or trampled. Sam and Raven spun around to see what no human or feline had ever seen in person. Standing at least twelve-feet tall above them and measuring at least thirty feet from head to tail was an Allosaurus, one of the largest-known carnivores that had ever walked the earth. Or, in this case, it was running straight for them.

Sam had a split second to react and push the button; but nothing happened. They were still there. Without even a second to think about moving, the dinosaur was upon them. His massive left foot slammed into the ground on their right side and his equally massive right foot whisked past them on their left, its claws dragging the ground. It passed them with such force that it pushed them to their right. They tumbled and rolled down into the giant left footprint it had impressed nearly three feet into the ground.

Raven did as all cats do, landing on his feet, but Sam landed on his back, knocking the breath out of him. They both whipped around to see if the giant was turning around. But its focus, thankfully, was on three smaller dinosaurs that were going to be lunch in a second or two.

Sam pushed the green button, but nothing happened again.

"Is it broken?" Raven asked.

"I don't know! I sure hope not. When old Al there gets done with his three appetizers, he may still need a main course. I think hiding would be a great idea about now."

Sam turned and started running in the opposite direction, away from the Allosaurus. Raven sped ahead of him. After running through the underbrush for about a quarter mile Raven slid to a stop and did a hard left.

"This way Sam, there's a cave."

A few feet off the animal trail they'd been on was a cave – really more of an overhang created by giant, exposed tree roots.

"Maybe we can hide here and regroup," Sam said.

"My thinking exactly," Raven said as he crept into the six-foot high root-ceiling. Sam followed him in and was surprised at how deep it was. The overhang actually did burrow deep under the tree.

Sam heard a shuffling from behind him and said, "Raven, stand still. We need to make as little noise as possible."

"Uh, boss, I've been a statue since we moved in. I haven't moved a muscle."

Shuffle, Shuffle, Shuffle.

"Well if you're not moving, who is?"

The cat and the boy turned their heads from the mouth of the overhang and peered back into the depths of the burrow. Three sets of faceless, golden eyes peered back at them. The eyes were at least five feet from the ground, so whatever they belonged to was pretty big.

"Sam, we are between the fabled rock and hard place here. It would really, really be good if you can get that remote working."

"Raven," Sam said with forced patience and hushed tones so as not to agitate whatever belonged to those eyes. "I do not have control of that. The darned device is not working. Savvy? I don't know why. *Capische?*"

"Yeah, I hear what you're saying but I don't like it."

"Well Raven, I don't like it any more than you, but when I push this button, nothing happens."

To demonstrate, Sam pushed the button. "See, nothing. I'll bet if I hit the home button nothing will happen. With that, he pushed the red button; a tunnel began forming and smoke started swirling. With speed that surprised them both, Raven jumped to Sam's side and slammed into him, nearly knocking him over screaming, "Hey, wait for me!"

"Hang on pal, here we go again."

Once again they spun down the long tunnel, this time even longer than the last. They weren't able to talk while they were in there because their words were literally ripped from their mouth and spread around the spirals of the tunnel, garbling them into oblivion. So all they could do was enjoy the ride and hope they ended up in a happy place. The good news was that once the time spiral started, they stayed together.

Finally, after what seemed like about ten minutes, the spiraling slowed, and the smoke began to clear. With a feeling that was equally elated and deflated, Sam saw that they were back home in his parents' basement lab. Fortunately, Dr. Molnikov had left after his attempt to kill Sam and steal the TimeCon.

Raven was joyous. "We made it! We made it! Nice going Sammy, I knew you could do it, you're a genius, I love ya' man!" Then he stopped when he saw the morose expression on Sam's face. "What? What is it Sam? What's wrong?"

"I'm happy to be home; but we still don't have Cici and Lily-Rose and I am reluctant to try to go back for them again until we get a better handle on how this all works."

"Oh, yeah, sorry, I got a bit excited, forgot about that. You're right. So what do we do now?"

Sam's shoulders slumped as he fell back onto the sofa. Raven jumped up next to him. They both sat there. Raven laid his head on Sam's leg and put his paw up on his knee.

"That's the problem Raven. I just don't know what to do," Sam said as he stroked Raven's soft, furry head. It had a calming effect on the boy and the animal.

Exhaustion took control and they both fell asleep.

20

SAM'S PARENTS FIND HOME

TONY AND AMANDA HAD NO IDEA that when they jumped from AD 280 they'd added another story to the Cartonia family's mystery collection when Valeria saw them disappear in her court yard amid swirling clouds and flashes of light.

Their 400-year time jump towards home was successful and they learned that the remote needed no more than five minutes to re-charge to the point that enabled them to jump again. With that knowledge, they learned to assess their situation as they were winding down in the time tunnel and quickly hide until their next jump.

It was exhausting. They were transiting nearly 2,000 years and even though they didn't have to do anything but stand there holding hands while they spun through time, it drained them. They suspected that there was a physiological reason for it, something at a molecular level that involved the mysterious green Amtonium and other factors they'd study if and when they got home.

Between jumps they would huddle in their hiding place and munch on the bread and cheese Valeria had so kindly packed for them. She had even included two corked bottles of wine, one red and one white.

"You know, this is sort of romantic," Amanda whispered in Tony's ear during one rest period when they'd landed in a marketplace filled with people, forcing them to huddle in a deserted alleyway between two mud-brick buildings. They sat on the ground with the bread and cheese on the unfolded cloth Valeria had wrapped them in. Both bottles of wine were uncorked; Tony preferred red; Amanda liked white.

"You really have to stretch the limits of romance to find this romantic," Tony said as he munched on a piece of cheese and took a swig from the wine bottle. "I mean, really, how did you reach that conclusion?"

Amanda's long, dark eyelashes batted pensively. She flipped her auburn hair over one shoulder and said in her sweetest southern drawl, "Well, we are on a once-in-a-lifetime adventure together, we have food and wine, we have to be touching at all times, so why not mix a little romance in there."

She was so appealing when she did that, Tony thought. He instantly forgot they were lost in time trying a hail-Mary attempt to get home. He was already sitting right next to her so he reached his hand around her waist, pulled her even closer and kissed her soft lips. "You make a very good point Mrs. Steelonni. Being with you makes even this strange trip we're on seem like a vacation. I do love you."

Then it was time to jump again. Tony had been adding 100 years each jump, so they were up to 800 year increments and he was reluctant to go above that. "No need to tempt fate," he told Amanda.

As they traveled, they could see the significant changes in their surroundings. Buildings, clothing, transportation and other aspects of society became more and more modernized until they began to recognize familiar Boston landmarks. Apparently, hitting the home button was actually bringing them from ancient Europe to modern-day Massachusetts. At one point they saw Boston Commons, a central park that had existed since 1634 and was the oldest park in the U.S. They lived near there so they knew they were getting closer and closer to home.

After two more jumps, on the next jump, as the tunnel wound itself down to a slow spiral and the smoke cleared, Amanda and Tony saw a sight that brought smiles to their faces. They were back in their home workshop and in front of them was their son, Sam, and his cat Raven, both fast asleep on the sofa.

The time tunnel was nearly noiseless so it didn't awaken the boy and cat, but when Amanda yelled "Alleluia!" it brought them off the sofa like two springs. As Sam woke up, he thought he was still dreaming because he thought he saw his parents, but he knew it wasn't a dream when they stepped forward and threw their arms around him and Raven.

"Mom, Dad, I can't believe it, where have you been, we've been looking for you all over the place, and time. What happened, how did you get back here…"

"Sam, slow down," Tony said. "We'll fill you in on all the details but just give us a few minutes to sit down and enjoy getting home and finding you and Raven here. I actually saw you in Rome, but that's part of the story so let us kick back and enjoy the moment."

"Absolutely, hey Sammy, how about you rustle us up some chow… I'll take some liver please…," Raven said with a smile and a wave of his paw and in a sophisticated dialect added, "Excuse me, do you have any grey poupon?"

Tony and Amanda stopped talking and watched with wide eyes and stunned looks on their faces. They looked at each other. "Did you hear that?" Tony asked Amanda, hoping she would say yes so he didn't have to add hallucinations to the list of things that time travel might inflict.

"Yes, and I am so happy you did too."

"Oh, yeah, surprise! You can finally understand cat language," Raven said, sitting down and raising his right paw with one clawed finger raised upward like a professor teaching a class. "It appears that one of the side-effects of time travel is that we can all communicate. Isn't that special?"

"It's true," Sam said. He originally thought that a person had to time jump with the animal to understand them, but apparently if the time tunnels intersected or paralleled along the way, that worked too. It was another unknown element of time travel they would have to study. "And, it seems that Raven has a pretty warped sense of humor to boot."

Tony and Amanda were silent, only their eyes moving back and forth from Sam to Raven as the unbelievable interchange between animal and human occurred right in front of them.

"Oh, this is so cool," Tony said, like a little kid who'd just seen his first model rocket blast off. "Can we understand all animals? Does it mean that anyone who time travels can understand anyone else, even if they speak another language? Can we talk to plants too?"

"Geez Tony, don't get carried away," his wife said. "We have plenty of time to experiment and study all these things and more, now that we have everybody safely back in one place."

"Yeah, about that...we have a problem," Sam said sheepishly, feeling like a little kid telling his parents he had tied the cans to the cat's tail. "We were looking for you and we found the other TimeCon and we were in ancient Rome and the soldiers were coming and I thought Cici was right there, but she wasn't, and I pushed the button, but it was too late, and she's still there, and her pet pig too. We tried to go back for her, but something's wrong with the TimeCon, I guess, and we kept ending up in the wrong place and the wrong time. She's still back there with the pig and I don't know what to do."

"So, Cici is now lost in time? Oh, this just keeps getting better and better," Tony said.

"Dad, it was an accident. She was there one minute and then this little girl pulled her into a house just as I pushed the button and she couldn't get to me."

"Wait, was the little girl named Maria Cartonia?" asked Amanda.

"Yes, I think so. She just popped out of a door and grabbed Cici. I think she was trying to help us because soldiers were coming."

"How long has she been missing?" Tony asked Sam.

"Hard to say, we've been in that time tunnel a while and I've kind of lost track, but I think, in normal time, a few hours."

"Has anyone told her parents?" Amanda asked him.

"No, we just got back and passed out. You woke us up. We haven't had time."

"OK, we've got to let them know and then they can help us. We have a ton of work to do if we're going to understand exactly what we're working with here," Tony said.

"No, dad, we've got to go back now! She could be in real danger. I am responsible for this. Her parents are going to hate me! We can't just leave her out there," Sam said in a desperate tone.

Tony put his hand on his son's shoulder and said quietly, but with conviction, "Sam, we're not saying that. Our highest priority will be to get her back. But if we go charging out there again, we'll all end up lost like last time and that won't help anybody."

Sam's mind was racing, his heart was pounding, and he wanted to scream. But when his father took his shoulder, it seemed to make it OK. He knew his dad was right. He knew they weren't even close to understanding this time travel phenomenon they'd discovered. It was amazing, it was frightening; it could change the world they knew. But getting a handle on the mechanics of time travel was going to take time. He would have to be patient.

"Oh, and one other problem you need to know about," Sam said, now addressing both his parents. "I believe Dr. Molnikov knows something about your discovery. On one time jump when Raven and I ended up back in the lab, he was here. We barely escaped. He shot at us with some kind of ray gun."

"He what?" Tony loudly interrupted, his paternal instinct and hot Italian temper dissipating his relaxed state of mind. "He was here… and he shot at you? He's gone too far this time. I'm going to find him and drag him to the police station myself!"

"Honey, I understand your anger, but I think our priority now is getting Cici and her pig back home," Amanda said, taking Tony by both shoulders and looking him square in the eyes. "We'll deal with Molnikov soon enough. Sam and Raven are here and safe, that's the important thing to remember."

Tony stopped, quelled by his wife's tone and touch. He looked into her eyes for several long seconds, unconsciously holding his breath. Exhaling slowly, he nodded and said, "You're right. We've got to…" Then he got a panicked look on his face as he sprinted to the big wall safe. He quickly dialed the combination, pulled open the heavy door and retrieved the smaller lock box containing the remaining Amtonium.

"I hope to heck he didn't get the last of our sample," he said, more to himself than anyone else. He dialed the combination on the smaller box and pulled open the lid just enough to see that the glowing green substance was still there.

"It's still here," he said, looking back at his family. "I wonder how much he knows…"

Amanda replied, "We'll find that out all in good time, Tony. Right now, we've got to get some rest so we can think clearly, then we've got to get some help and find Cici."

Turning her gaze to Sam, she saw the pain and guilt in his eyes. She said, "Sam, Cici is a very smart girl, very capable of taking care of herself," Amanda reassured Sam. "Her parents know you and they know you would do anything to get her back. Once they hear the circumstances they will understand. We're all going to have to work together to get this done. We all need to be ready to immerse ourselves in this."

Sam held up his hands palms out and said, "OK, ok, I get it, but I need to be the one to tell them. I need to look them in the eyes. They need to know how much their daughter means to me and how sorry I am." Amanda nodded agreement.

Everybody jumped when Charger burst through the door and yelled, "You guys are back! I'm really glad because I was running out of ideas on how to help you." Akamaru padded in behind him, sat down and said in a deep, monotone voice, "Well, look what the cat dragged in," not meaning to be funny but making everyone smile anyway.

Sam quickly filled Charger in on the plight of Cici and Lily-Rose and the need to work on a plan to get them back.

There was a long silence as everyone absorbed the enormity of the task before them. Then, from the back of the sofa came a gravelly voice, sounding like a Marine Corps drill instructor talking to a platoon of new recruits.

"OK ladies and gentlemen, I suggest you get your giant brains and your opposable thumbs into gear and start solving all these problems because we are now fully engaged in Operation Retrieve Cici and Lily-Rose. It's time to bring them home!" said Raven, standing stoically on his hind legs astride the back of the sofa, his front paws clenched

Sam's parents, Akamaru, Sam and Charger are amused at Raven's antics as they begin the planning to rescue Cici and Lily-Rose and bring them back home from ancient Rome.

into fists, his knuckles resting on his hips, looking stern. Then he gave them all a smile and a wink and said, "Bet you folks would never have guessed I could do that, did ya'?"

There was a long pause, and then they all burst out laughing. Raven's humor was the catalyst to set them in motion. From this point forward they had one shared goal: figure out how to get Cici and Lily-Rose home.

End, Book One
Essence of Time Trilogy, Book Two, Coming Soon

ACKNOWLEDGMENTS

THE PROCESS OF WRITING A BOOK and getting it published isn't easy and it's not a one-person show; it's a team effort. I'd like to thank a few special people who helped me usher this book from concept to finished product. First, my wife, Ellen, who read my initial draft, made observations, and shared her thoughts—but most importantly encouraged me to continue by saying, "I think this is really good!" Next, my older brother, Tim, who is a prolific writer, motivated me by his actions when he wrote and published a book about our family growing up on a farm in Wisconsin. I am grateful for the help and encouragement of a writing group I was part of in Bay Minette, Alabama, led by author Sylvia Weiss Sinclair. Their ideas and feedback helped push me through the first chapters of the book and gave me hope that the book would be well received. Editor and publisher Harley Patrick of Paloma Books was patient and helpful as he navigated me through the unfamiliar waters of book preparation and publishing. The staff at GYBI (Get Your Books Illustrated) were exceptionally supportive and effective as they helped turn my concepts into living, breathing illustrations that helped visualize a few key scenes in the book. Last, I thank you, the reader. I hope you enjoy it, maybe learn a thing or two; but, above all, have a good "time" reading it. And I hope you'll join me for Book Two in the "Essence of Time Trilogy," coming soon.

RANDY GADDO DEVELOPED HIS WRITING SKILLS as a United States Marine Corps Combat Correspondent. For twenty years he served as a photojournalist, editor, press chief and media officer, telling the Marine Corps story to the public. He has been published in many military and civilian newspapers, magazines, and other publications. He now is a freelance writer. "The Essence of Time Trilogy" is his first entry into writing books. He read books as a child, and read to his children when they were young, and knows how important the plots and characters in books can be. He writes with the reader in mind, whether he or she is a young reader, a parent reading to their child, or an educator or librarian choosing a book for young readers. Randy currently lives in Athens, Georgia, with his wife, Ellen, and two cats— Rouse (pronounced ROUS EE – named after Ronda Rousey, the WWE woman fighter) and Scooter. They have three grown children.

Made in the USA
Columbia, SC
30 April 2022

59729379R00078